Everyone
wants to be a winner

Winning is the goal, but before you can win the championship, you must learn how to deal with defeat. For Jeff Eben, at age 16, his teammates, friends, family, and coaches were suddenly swept off the practice field and into the real world, where victory and defeat are respecters of no man.

As you read this book, know that Jeff Eben is the best of the best, and the best I have ever had the privilege to coach. The Bible says in 1st Corinthians 13:13, "there are three things: "faith, hope, and love. The greatest of these is love." I love Jeff Eben. Let this book be your guide to finding the wins in your defeats.

Jack Bohan,
Coach

Design, Layout and Graphics
Created by:
Ernie (HERGIE) Hergenroeder
hergie@sbcglobal.net

*H*ope and Love are gifts that can change the world. When I received them, it allowed me to build a life out of a type of rubble that I never thought I'd have to experience. When I gave them, I found it changed the lives of young people and provided them the strength needed to go after the rewards life has to offer. When I built a community around those two words, things happened that defied expectations. Hope and Love have the ability to challenge the best in all of us and unlock the limits of our potential. At least it did for me and the students and staff at Clovis East High School. In fact, these two powerful words provided me the tools necessary to embark on a journey that took me from the bottom of a lake in 1977 to the principal's office of a school I built from scratch. I share my story as a celebration of life and the belief that we all need to be reminded of both the little victories and big wins that surround us every day.

"How Many Wins Have YOU Had Today?"
is an imprint of Garden of Eben Publishing Co.

Published by
Garden of Eben Publishing Co.
Fresno, California
Copyright © 2006 Jeff Eben
Fresno, California
All rights reserved.
Printed on Demand
Third Printing - June 2017
10 9 8 7 6 5 4 3 2 1

Library of Congress Control Number: 2006906698
Jeff Eben
The story of **"How Many Wins Have YOU Had Today?"**
/ written by Jeff Eben
Design & Layout by Ernie "Hergie" Hergenroeder
Summary: An autobiography of Jeff Eben and his rise
from disasters to success.
ISBN: 0-9777666-0-9 (Hardcover)
ISBN 1547204567 (Paperback)
Copyright to include all characters, design & content

HOW MANY WINS HAVE **YOU** HAD TODAY?

A book about winning

by

Jeff Eben

INDEX

To The Winners In My Life:

To Mom – *When I was 8 and fell during a race, you ran onto the track and made me get up and finish even though I was crying and bleeding. Who knew then how smart that move would become . . . thank you.*

To my brothers, Jon and Scott – *Thanks for the countless hours in the driveway. You taught me to compete to win.*

To my sister Suzi – *you made yourself into the biggest winner of us all. Thanks for being my role model.*

To the students and staff of Clovis High School's Class of 1979 – *Thanks for taking care of me when I needed it the most.*

To my pals *(you know who you are)* – *you showed me what love really means.*

To Michelle P., Lori, and Moody – *Your willingness to love me was an incredible gift.*

To my Dad – *Thanks for finding your way home. It was cool.*

To Coach Jack Bohan – *all the wins in my life start with you. I will owe you forever.*

And to Michelle, Jared, and Noelle Eben . . . *I consider myself a winner because of you.*

Special Thanks To:

Mike and Kenlynn Nelson *for their sincere help on this project.*

Joe and Diane Prevendar *for your cheerleading and editing. Diane, your effort made this happen.*

This is a book about winning.

Coach Jack Bohan

FOREWORD

As a football coach, my class room was the practice field. Friday night's game was the test for lessons learned. Across America, practice and playing fields have proven to be the place where young people learn in a laboratory of life experiences. Athletes bring to sports all they are: physical stature, mental abilities, integrity, and character. They come with hopes and dreams they have in their minds from early childhood. This, a highly competitive and focused environment, where expectations are held high, learning is swift, excitement great, with energy and confidence that they can make a difference. The experiential learning opportunities are endless. Winning is the goal, but before you can win the championship, you must learn how to deal with defeat. For Jeff Eben, at age 16, his teammates, friends, family, and coaches were suddenly swept off the practice field and into the real world, where victory and defeat are respecters of no man.

I was Jeff's coach. On October 2, 1977, my life and all I professed to believe in were suddenly put to test. I believe in a loving God who put us on earth to find our way. His test would teach me about courage, strength, friendship, patience, kindness, faith, hope and most of all love. My whole teaching strategy is built around the power of words and how they build or destroy confidence and lead us to success or failure. There seem to be faith filled words, which bring hope and an attitude of "I can," or fear filled words, which tear down and develop a negative "I can't" attitude. We all respond to the talk of others and even more so to our own self talk. My teaching method revolved around the following thesis: Words trigger pictures, which trigger feelings, emotions, and establish our attitudes, which direct our choices and lead to a destiny of success or failure. The attitude we bring with us, in

7

the face of tragedy and defeat, will determine our destiny as we exercise our power of choice. I have a habit of saying: "It's a great day today; it's the first day of forever". This belief is imbedded deep in my soul.

This story is about a 16 year old boy with a bright future as a student athlete and his road to victory over what could have been a devastating defeat. It's about all the people who were there for him and his family. It's about a battle between hope and no hope. It is a story that demonstrates that within every defeat, no matter how bad, victory can be found. It's about a love that dominates everything, one that can be felt, and a love that never loses. It is about a real champion who discovered the secret to victory in the midst of defeat by focusing on personal victories.

On the practice field at Clovis High School, a healthy teaching environment was created. It emphasized the positive or little wins, and stressed the expectation of doing little things correctly in order to complete the task at hand. Jeff and his fellow offensive lineman worked hard on the "little things" and began to develop the attitude that they could win any and all battles they encountered. Scrimmages against the defense would trigger comments like, "What was your win? Great step, that's just like you!!" If things did not go the way the coaches expected, one would hear, "That's not like you, Jeff, but great effort, your first step was excellent!! Is there a win in there someplace?" By constantly focusing on things done well, confidence grew and expectations became reality. Our offensive lineman knew that if their play went sour, as it sometimes does, the situation could change if each individual would look for and focus on the good, and the positive, while having the attitude of, "That's just like us to overcome". A team will pull together when they help a teammate find a victory from a personal defeat. That kind of love moved all of us to understand that it was a matter of time when the big picture would clear to our favor. Jeff and his fellow teammates soon learned that the battles on the field did not always go to the stronger or faster man, but swings in favor of the one who is focused on the little wins that take place in spite of the surrounding circumstances.

One of my favorite drills in football for offensive lineman is one-on-one. This is a situation where two large bags are placed flat on the ground about three yards apart parallel to each other. An offensive lineman, with a running back behind him, faces one defensive lineman. It's either you or him. On the snap count the O-lineman strikes into the D-lineman and the back runs into the hole created by the O-lineman. Once contact is made and the fur flies, opportunities for teaching abound. It allows one to realize how "the little things" are important to winning. A boy has to dig deep to find his win between the bags as a defender has stuffed him into the hole and tackled the running back. Being stuffed is not a good thing; however confidence grows as the boy realizes and discovers the small win in his defeat and builds on it. The next time the fur flies, the defensive lineman is stuffed and the back runs free, then the "I can" attitude prevails.

Jeff became good at this drill. He grew to focus on the "little things" and his wins to follow. Little did I know that someday he would inspire many to understand the importance of winning and help us to overcome defeat. Jeff changed my life and inspires me every day. When I think of him and all who were and still are involved in his life, I realize the importance of one life, finding a win and discovering what real love is.
There are times in life when we are faced with situations which overwhelm us, put us down and very much out. These are obstacles which we do not see any way of overcoming. This is the time for people with understanding and love to step up. Jeff's teammates, friends, family, and teachers, did just that. They came forward with a demonstration of love and hope that rose above a hopeless situ-

9

ation. Together, whether knowingly or unknowingly, they were able to move a mountain of despair and discover a love and hope which always finds a way.

On a visit to our Naval Academy in Annapolis, I had the honor of meeting a decorated Vietnam veteran. This Marine Lt. Col. was an instructor there. I asked him what makes strong leaders who never give up when faced with failure and defeat. He said the Academy purposefully makes each day a struggle for cadets. It is the struggle that one faces each day that shapes the character of every cadet. When you read this book and look at Jeff's life, you will not see a wheelchair, occupied by a disabled person. You will learn about a boy who has great character, is full of courage and hope, and a competitive spirit that won't stay defeated. Travel with him as he grows into manhood finding win after win after win. Go with him as he describes the struggles he finds himself dealing with, leads past the nay-sayers, unbelievers and hopeless, into a life full of hope and love. A life that to this day will not be denied.

While coaching football I had the opportunity to teach many young men. As you read this book, know that Jeff Eben is the best of the best, and the best I have ever had the privilege to coach. In 1st Corinthians 13vr 13, the Bible says that there are three things: "faith, hope, and love. The greatest of these is love." I love Jeff Eben. Let this book be your guide to finding the wins in your defeats.

Coach Jack Bohan

November, 2003

*I*t was cold on this particular Friday night, but I didn't feel it. Being paralyzed from the chest down wasn't the reason as I'm usually pretty sensitive to extreme temperatures. This was all about excitement and, on this day after Thanksgiving, I was painfully close to fulfilling a dream. I had parked myself in my wheelchair in the end zone of Floyd B. Buchanan Stadium while my football team played for its first Valley Championship. I know it shouldn't be that important, but I was the principal of a brand new high school and winning would be a crowning moment for the new community I had tried to create. A crowd of about six thousand people had gathered for this contest, which featured the top two teams in the San Joa-quin Valley of Central California. Though not Texas, our high school football games are huge community events and our program was in its infancy, making our appear-ance in the Championship game a great story.

Actually, for me to be there at all was a bit of a surprise. Growing up I was sure I would play my way to champi-onship glory. As the youngest in a family of athletes, I watched my brothers play on teams that never quite won the ring. Going back even further, I ran countless side-lines as a young child while my father coached teams that had great seasons, but never brought home the title. I was the final hope and since my school was a football powerhouse in our area, I liked my chances. Fate inter-vened, however, and my high school career was cut short. My life took a far different path and I learned the game of life was far more painful and arduous than any day on the gridiron. Strangely enough, this night brought my recovery full circle and a football championship was more than an ironic testimony to a philosophy I had learned as

11

a teenager that reminded me to always count my blessings and believe in the power of the heart.

After ten years in education as a teacher and an administrator, I was selected to lead the physical and philosophical creation of Clovis East High School, which opened with only ninth graders in the fall of 1999. We added a class each year, and in June of 2003, that initial group of students became our first graduates. They took their lumps over the first four years and constantly strove for credibility. Here it was only six months after saying goodbye to that class of young people who had become my friends, and we were competing on the largest stage California provides for high school athletics. Our team had a storybook season entering the big game with a record of 11 wins and 1 loss. The good times included a win that made national news when we traveled to Southern California and shocked the prep football world by upsetting perennial power Long Beach Poly. We won by a score of 17-13 on their home turf; where they hadn't lost since 1985, the year many of our seniors were born. The bad news was that our only loss of the season came against Clovis West High School, our cross-town rivals. They were another traditional power annually ranked as one of the top teams in our state. They whipped us good too, and taunted us with chants of "overrated" as we walked off the field after that loss. Yes, they were our opponents this night, and if we were going to take home the trophy, we had to find a way to over come their reputation, skill, confidence, and the memory of that earlier contest.

Like me, our kids were used to being underdogs. Because of being new, many of the top scholars and athletes in our school's area exercised their option to attend the other, more established schools rather than risk the growing pains of coming to an unproven educational institution. Our students had a feeling of being the kids that nobody wanted and we were in a constant search for respect and acceptance. From the first day the school opened, it was the job of our staff to make our community believe in itself and, hopefully, build some trust between the school and our constituents. As hard as we tried, and as far out as we reached, we needed to become winners in some way to be credible. For the first four years wins were few and far between, but we had a lot of which to be proud. Still, the excitement built by this successful young football team had done more to build pride in our school than any speech I could have made or test scores we could have published. We had become the talk of the town and, all of a sudden, it was cool to be a Clovis East Timberwolf. A win tonight would start a party that might last awhile. Nobody, though, thought we had a chance against this team. Nobody, that is, except us.

The game had gone better than our wildest dreams could have hoped. Tracy, our sophomore running back, had been fabulous during our playoff run. He had to fill in for our outstanding senior half back that had gone down with an injury in the first round (actually the first play) of the post season. Tracy broke loose for a sixty-five yard run on the night's third play putting us in scoring position. We finished the deal and before the crowd had warmed their seats, we were leading 7-0.

Our euphoria was brief as our opponent scored midway through the second quarter. Luckily for us, they missed the extra point and we held a slim 7-6 lead late at the half. Their touchdown brought them to life, though, and they drove deep into our territory with less than a min-ute before halftime. As they appeared ready to score, I sensed the doubt creeping into our collective conscious-ness. If nothing else, it had sure found its way into my brain. At that moment, as if on cue, our standout senior linebacker, who had lived through the lean years, stepped in front of a pass in the end zone and was off to the races. After an eighty-yard run, Edwin ran out of gas at about the twenty-yard line. He not only stopped Clovis West's drive, but also gave us a chance in the closing seconds of the half to build our lead. Though we weren't able to score, we went to the locker room with the advantage and something even more important; we had hope. I have always believed that hope would be enough, and I taught that lesson to my students. Tonight, however, would be the ultimate test of that theory.

Apparently, Clovis West High School didn't care about my beliefs. This school, for which I had once worked, wanted a title of their own. They had won many in the past, but this particular group of students had lost the championship game the previous year, and they were hungry . . . and confident. It was a little awkward for me, though. Years previous, I had been principal of an elementary school and many of the West kids were former students of mine who I loved dearly. On second thought, it wasn't that awkward. They gave no love the first time we played, and I wanted this win badly for all the students and families who came to our school and put up with the jokes and insults about being new.

Anyway, Clovis West took the second-half kickoff and drove down the field rather easily. They were starting to assert their dominance and wound up on our five-yard line ready to assume the lead right in front of me. I moved my wheelchair to get out of the way as a touchdown was seconds away. The collective will of our kids made our defense dramatically stiffen, and Clovis West settled for a field goal. Sure, they took a 9-6 lead, but we achieved a moral victory with an impressive goal-line stand. For the rest of the third quarter, the game was played in the middle of the field with both teams failing to seriously threaten. The one thing I noticed, though, was that the hits got louder and louder, and we were the team giving the punishment. As the fourth quarter started, I knew we were in good shape. We had kept the game close giving us a chance at the upset.
More importantly, though, I didn't get the sense that our opponents were enjoying themselves. We had weakened

their will. Our kids on the field and in the stands were starting to believe and the tension that had built was turning to confidence. It was clear that four years of fighting for respect and credibility had taken its toll and we were ready to claim a deserved prize of our own.

We finally drove deep into scoring territory but were stopped. There was still plenty of time, but we had to score and hadn't done so since the first minute of the game. Clovis West took over on downs and threw a pass over the middle on their first play of the drive. As their outstanding quarterback released the ball, he was hit hard and the ball floated above the intended target. When the ball came to rest in the arms of Jesse, one of our undersized defensive backs, our season came into clear focus. We had the ball in scoring position and had a chance to win. A touchdown here would be huge and as our defensive back handed the referee the ball after the interception, he also handed our community the opportunity for which we had waited. We needed to seize this moment.

Sure enough, we completed a huge pass to our tight end giving us first and goal about six yards from the goal line and about sixteen yards from my lap. This time I wasn't wheeling out of the way. I could feel it coming and I wanted to be as close as possible. Again we called on our sophomore running back, and when he tumbled into the end zone, it was bedlam. Nobody even noticed that we went for two and made it giving us a 15-9 lead in the waning minutes. If our defense could keep them out of the end zone, we would win. As potent as they were, we were flying high and I liked our chances. Their now desperate passing attempts fell incomplete and our backs delivered crunching hits that silenced their fans and had our crowd hysterical. We forced them to punt and we took possession with about three minutes remaining. All we needed was one first down and we would be able to run out the clock.

Our crowd was holding its breath, our team and coaches closed ranks, and our victory song "Ain't No Mountain High Enough" was in the CD player. As soon as we had the game in hand, I would give the nod to my staff, and a beautiful chorus of some three thousand of my closest friends would break out into a song that we had sung eleven times prior to this moment. I had the feeling the notes would be a little louder on this chilly evening. First, though, we needed that one first down.

I left my perch and started wheeling my electric chair down the sideline in front of our crowd and closer to our team. I wanted to immerse myself in the champions' rituals of hugs, backslapping, and ice showers. With one first down, we would have all of those, but a penalty put our celebration on hold. The clock was ticking. Now under two minutes, but with second down and twenty yards to go, we were certain to have to punt and hold them one more time. As I continued my roll down the sideline, I took my eyes off of the field. A roar erupted and when I looked up, Tracy was running right at me and clear of every defender. His gallop to the end zone was surreal, and as our team rushed to mob him, the officials were standing at about midfield waving their arms. Apparently, our young workhorse had stepped out of bounds, negating the clinching touchdown. Our party was on hold and I was about to be sick. Luckily, he gained enough yards to give us a chance at that elusive first down. It was **third and five,** and in one play, we would know if we would do what seemed impossible, or give a great team another chance.

I had seen and heard of the impossible before and had to smile at the moment. My entire family had come to the game as a quasi-vindication for the many close calls in years past. My father had re-entered our lives after thirty years of indifference and sat in the stands riddled with cancer hoping to capture one last moment of glory. As we readied for this third-down play, I knew that the entire Eben family had their own reasons to appreciate this event. I'm sure they all paused as I did to acknowl-edge the irony of what might happen in the next few sec-onds. We had been waiting for this first down for twenty-six years. Could this be the moment? For me, I smiled because an old coach that came to my rescue many years earlier was about to be right . . . again.

I

Learning About the Power of Hope and Love Saved My Life. . .

August, 1977

*T*hese were the brightest days of my young life. I was a junior at Clovis High School and had the world on a string. I had been voted class president by my peers and was thoroughly enjoying the school scene. I had a great bunch of pals, a beautiful girlfriend named Kim, and a sixteen-year-old's pride and joy – my driver's license. In my life, though, the best thing going was I was finally playing on the varsity football team. I grew up on the sidelines every Friday night, but this was different. I was no longer the son or little brother of someone on the team, I wore the uniform and I was sure that life could get no better. Besides, I had a major knee injury during the last game of my sophomore year on the junior varsity. I was told my playing days were over, but I refused to accept that, and I went through two knee surgeries and daily therapies with our school's athletic trainer to prove the doctor wrong. After months of sweating, whirlpools, and trying to get a normal range of motion in my right knee, spring football began in May and I was cleared to play. I had been through hell to be on that team and I was going to make the most of my time.

I reported to practice in the best shape of my life. I breezed through the two weeks of two-a-days and was ready to contribute. At our school, the offensive line was the glory position, and we were hand picked to join this elite group. Our line coach was a guy named Jack Bohan, a personality to say the least. He was considered the best line coach around, but that was a small part of his legend. A teacher and counselor, he was the most visible force on our campus. He ran the Fellowship of Christian Athletes and it was THE club to join. He hosted Bible studies in his home every Wednesday night for as long as I was aware, and there were nights that the

19

crowd of students who came to hear him talk about God numbered in the hundreds. Coach Bohan was also the master of positive thinking and everything he said was purposeful and intended to make you believe you could accomplish any task or goal you attempted. Playing for him was considered an honor, and I was in an elite group. I was proud, but things weren't going as I had hoped.

I'd always been one of the top players and had been a starter on both offense and defense through Pop Warner, junior high, and my early high school years. On our varsity, you didn't play both ways, so I was a center on the offense. Unfortunately for me, our team returned its center from the last year and despite all my efforts, I was on the bench for the first time in my life. To make matters worse, we started the year as one of the top ranked teams in the Valley, and were underachieving big time. We tied our first game and lost our second. So, when we were preparing for our final non-conference game before starting league play, we were feeling the heat both literally and figuratively.

The last week of September was typically hot in Fresno, and this year was no exception. I was feeling better about my role and was now playing on special teams. I was also starting to take turns at other positions on the line and was beginning to establish myself as a valuable utility player. I knew in my heart my time to be a varsity starter was near, and I was ready. Unfortunately, Coach Bohan wasn't enjoying my personal growth. I doubt he had ever been winless at this point in the season as a player or as a coach, so he was working us harder and yelling at us a little louder each day. Part of what made him great was his total freedom to share his emotions, so we were used to his being pretty animated. This particular Wednesday, though, was something we hadn't seen. It was the last day of full practice for the week before a light workout on Thursday and game day on Friday. It was well over 100 degrees and we were uninspired, to say the least.

Coach decided that the reason for our lethargy was the immaturity of the juniors, whom he lovingly dubbed "Panty-Waste Juniors." He started to go off on a tirade and decided he would demonstrate how to block while foaming at the mouth. He turned his hat and whistle around, never a good sign, and looked for the closest "PWJ," which today was me. He got in his stance and asked me to do the same. We were nose to nose, but I was in full gear and he was in shorts and a T-shirt. Besides that, I was young, strong, and in the best shape of my life. He was in his forties and hadn't played since being a Small College All-American at Fresno State in 1961. I looked in his eyes and knew I had no chance. He asked me to step to a gap, which I did. He, however, stepped the other way and fell flat on his face. I could swear I heard the Clint Eastwood whistle from "The Good, The Bad, and The Ugly" as he got up, got back in his stance, and told me, "Just come straight at me." What happened next was a blur, but it stopped practice and became a spectacle. He knocked me around and around, talking trash at me the whole time. I was really ticked and totally humiliated, but no worse for wear. I put my hand on my chinstrap and was about to quit on the spot. Catching my eye, though, was my friend and our team captain Mike Lamb. Big Mike put his hand out giving me the universal gesture to calm down. I took a deep breath and went back to practice, but I looked at Coach very differently. Is he the man I thought or is he a modern day version of Dr. Jekyll and Mr. Hyde?

Our game Friday was another bad night. We lost and had the misfortune of being the first Clovis team in recent history to go winless in the preseason. A suburb of Fresno in the heart of the San Joaquin Valley, Clovis is a small, close-knit community that revolved around its school system and promoted itself as having a "Western way of life." For many, Clovis High football was a great source of civic pride and losing was not accepted. Our futility was becoming embarrassing, and as we gathered at

Me-N-Ed's Pizza, our usual post-game hangout that resembled a scene out of "American Graffiti," we knew changes were coming for the team. Deep down, I was selfishly excited because I expected to be in the mix after the coaches made adjustments. In my heart of hearts, I knew that Monday would begin my life as a starting player for the Clovis Cougars, and I'd be ready. My best pal Randy, his girlfriend Wendi, Kim and I left the pizza parlor and parked out in the country. Kim made me feel much better, and I headed home to rest for the weekend. I knew that the next week would be the biggest of my life. I was ill prepared to be so right.

I was awakened by the telephone late on Sunday morning. I'm a notoriously late sleeper, so any call before noon would catch me snoring. It was the second of October but hot enough to feel like July. On the other end of the phone was my friend Dale who offered me a day of water skiing at Lake Millerton, a few miles from my trailer park. I spent the summer with Dale and his family up in Washington and Idaho where they were bitten by the water sports bug. Dale's folks bought a beautiful new speedboat and I was excited to join them for the day. My mom was working as a nurse to make ends meet and times were tough for us. My friends were great to me, though, and I never missed out on anything. I always jumped at the chance to do something fun. So even though I couldn't get a hold of my mom to ask permission, I was soon picked up and on my way to the lake.

To say the day was spectacular was an understatement. The sky was clear, the sun was blazing, and the lake's traffic was minimal. As we proceeded to take turns being towed by Dale's dad, I was embarrassed by my ineptitude on skis. Dale, his older sister Leeanne, and younger brother Curt were all graceful as they single skied back and forth across the water. They would jump the wake and spray water with their feet as they changed direction; it was very cool to watch. I, on the other hand, was

22

a complete clod. I would put a death grip on the rope and be pulled on two skis, never moving side to side for fear of falling. My ego was large, though, and by lunch I'd had enough. After we ate I was going to learn to single ski, no way around it. I knew I wasn't ready, but that seemed un-important. I'd take a couple of attempts and have it mas-tered by the time we left for home. I started this quest at about one in the afternoon. At four, I was still in the water and my sinuses were now clear, but I still was un-able to stand up behind the boat for as little as a second on the one ski. At least I was providing comedic relief to Dale's family for the day.

We were ready to call it quits when the competitor in me asked for one more chance. My request was granted, but someone in the group recommended a different tac-tic. It was suggested I ski around the lake on two skis in a circle. Then, when I passed the start point, which was in a little cove by the shore, I'd kick one ski off and let the boat pull me as long as I could last on the other ski. It sounded like a great plan, and we were off within sec-onds. I was a model of true perfection as I circled around the lake waiting for the moment I could make the big drop-off. It was less than a minute before the boat pulled me in the cove, parallel to the shore. It was time, and I pulled my foot out of the boot and released the ski as planned. I was up and skiing on one ski feeling like the best athlete in the world. The boat started to turn slightly out of the cove and into the main part of lake. The turn-ing whipped me to the side of the craft, and I was travel-ing at a high rate of speed. Since the cove was U-shaped and I didn't have the skill to negotiate the turn, it was time to abort the mission before I wound up crashing into the rocks on the rapidly approaching shoreline. Instead, I fell head first into the water in a diving motion and in a split-second; I knew I was in trouble.

Apparently, the water was much shallower than we knew and directly under the surface were boulders and tree stumps waiting to be challenged. My head hit the first object traveling at about 35-40 miles per hour. From there, everything moved in slow motion. I vividly remember the sound of crunching bones in my neck and the feeling of my body going limp. My odyssey was not complete, though, as I tumbled and tumbled over the water until I came to rest within ten feet of the shore. With each tumble I smacked my head on something unbelievably hard. As I lay face down on the lake's surface, the pain was incredible, but the reality that I was going to drown made my neck a secondary concern. I was sure that in the time it would take the boat to circle close enough to reach me, I'd be gone. It was surreal.

I have no idea why or how, but I flipped over to my back and could see the sky. More to the point, I could breathe, though it was painful. I'm not sure if the life jacket I was wearing saved me or God decided it wasn't my time. Either way, I'm very thankful.

I knew immediately that I was paralyzed. I laid in the water and screamed for it not to be true, but I knew the score. When my friends reached me, they were overcome by the blood. I'd ripped open the top of my head pretty good, and they knew I needed help fast. They carefully placed me in the boat, supporting my head the whole time. I was screaming in pain and fear, though I'm not sure which caused the loudest yell. When we arrived at the boat ramp, medical personnel had already arrived. They bandaged my head and braced my neck for the twenty-minute ambulance ride to the hospital. All I could think of was I did not want to be paralyzed. After all, I'd worked hard for the team and this was going to be the week I was rewarded with playing time. As the ambulance pulled away from the lake, I didn't know what was ahead. I did know, though, that my life would never be the same.

October, 1977

As soon as the ambulance arrived, I was met by my mom and the emergency room staff at the hospital. Being a nurse, my mom was well aware of the possibilities associated with head and neck injuries. Being a mother, however, of four children who were athletes and a little on the daring side, she was pretty sure this would be another short stop in the emergency room before we headed home for dinner. As soon as she saw me come out on the gurney, she knew this wasn't a stitches and Band-Aid injury. All I could tell her was "Mom, I don't want to be paralyzed!" There wasn't much she could say, but certainly the reality of what was ahead had not materialized.

The emergency room staff tugged on my shoulders and rolled me around for what seemed like hours. The pulling was designed to give the X-ray technician a clean shot at his target. The more they yanked my shoulders down, the louder I screamed in agony. My neck was throbbing and the pain was unbearable. I also could feel tingling in my arms and legs that was like nothing I'd ever felt before. The tingling was the worst because I couldn't feel anything else, and I was starting to panic. I'm not sure why, but I knew what a broken neck was and I knew that an injury in that area could make you paralyzed. My fear was incomprehensible. The longer I was poked, prodded, pulled on, and prayed over, the more I knew that something very bad was happening. While it took forty-eight stitches to close the massive, C-shaped gash on the top of my head, that wasn't the entire story. I had broken my neck in three places and had major spinal cord damage. I would need surgery and traction, and the staff prepared my mother and, by this time, my sister Suzi for the possibility of my not surviving. My brothers, Jon and Scott, had moved in together over on the Central Coast and it

27

would be several hours before they were notified. My father had left us some five years earlier and also lived in the Central Coast area with his new wife, Pam. We had a decent relationship, but he wasn't around much. Dad was always the life of the party with a booming voice and a good joke, but he was not that interested in our daily lives and was never much on fatherly wisdom or advice. I had learned not to rely on him for parental support, and this would be no different.

I will never forget the feeling of the two metal tongs that were screwed into each side of my skull near my temple. I could hear the skin rip and the sound of metal on bone as each bolt entered my head. Once secure, they tied thirty-five pounds of weight to the bolts and placed me in a bed called a striker frame. This traction made it impossible to move my head and allowed the nurses to rotate the bed every two hours to avoid getting pressure sores. All I knew is it hurt like hell and didn't make sleeping very easy. As soon as I hit the room on that first night, though, I was out.

The intensive care unit of the hospital was very dark and eerily quiet. If I was looking for inspiration, I wasn't going to find it in the little room that would be my home for the next two weeks. One little beam came from a small fixture in the ceiling providing about as much radiance as you'd get from a small flashlight. With the nursing staff checking on you every fifteen minutes and never speaking above a whisper, this location didn't strike me as a place to get well. It seemed like a good spot to be right before you die, and that possibility was not lost on me.

I was checked on often but don't recall waking up until sometime in the middle of the night. I vividly remember the brief second of joy when I thought the whole day had been a bad dream. Soon the fear and pain came and it was all very real. It's funny the thoughts that occupied my mind in the early hours and days. There I was close

28

to death and with no feeling from the neck down, and I was in a hurry. I really needed to get this over with so I could get back to practice. I had no intention of missing our first league game and the people in the hospital needed to understand that. It was that first Tuesday when Dr. Slater, a neurologist, met with me and explained the severity of my injury. For a young athlete, the worst possible scenario was about to come to life.

"This is your spinal cord," he said rather matter of factly while holding a diagram of a skeleton, "and these are the vertebrae in your neck. You crushed your spinal cord at the fourth, fifth, and sixth vertebrae and you are paralyzed from the neck down."

Though I wasn't surprised, I was not quite in touch with reality when I responded.

"Will I be able to play Friday night?" I asked.

I don't remember his answer, but it hardly mattered. I do remember him explaining that I needed emergency surgery to try to repair the bones in my neck or I would not recover any movement in my arms at all. The operation was dangerous but a no-brainer. I agreed to it and even had to acknowledge the ever-increasing reality that I might have to miss one game.

The surgery went off without a hitch, but my body was starting to reject the trauma. First, I developed something called ICU psychosis. Basically, I lost my mind. Your brain can handle so much, and with all of the turmoil I was in and the fistful of powerful drugs I swallowed by the hour, I began to hallucinate regularly. I saw things, heard voices, and held full conversations with imaginary people. I became verbally abusive to anyone who tried to convince me that I was not living in reality. It was a very difficult time for everybody, made worse by the fact that I was just plain mean. Luckily, my

Aunt Mary was a nursing administrator at this hospital and oversaw every minute of my care. She had worked there for years and had been by my side through an earlier broken arm and leg. The intensity level was quite a bit higher this time, but she was a rock of stability. The psychosis was unbelievably frightening when I was lucid and she made sure a psychologist saw me before it got worse. He was able to treat me and, after about a week of this nuttiness, it went away. It was followed though by a nasty bleeding ulcer that had me crapping all over the bed about every ten minutes. It was bad enough that the nurses had to call my mom back to the hospital in the middle of the night on one occasion. When she arrived, my stomach had filled with blood and was fully distended. She had to approve a procedure where they drilled into my belly to alleviate the pressure. It worked, but I was finding this new life less than enjoyable.

The worst part of the ICU experience, though, was that brutally awful striker frame. Every two hours I had to be turned, which sounded harmless. That process called for a cage-like device that attached to the bed that kept me secure as I rotated like a pig on a barbecue until I was facing the floor. I would stay in that position until it was time to turn again. It had two cushions made of something very rough. The pads were about a foot long and maybe three to four inches wide. One went across my forehead, the other across my chin. Every time I turned, the material rubbed my skin so raw it bled. I would have to lie facing the floor for two-hour periods, and the wounds got bigger every shift. All anyone could see was my face from the eyes to the mouth. One of the nursing aides liked to call me "Rocket Man" every time I suited up, which did actually make me laugh. As soon as the turning started, though, the smiles went away. Apparently, this type of bed was new and most of the staff didn't know how it worked. They learned on me. It never failed, however, that something would go wrong. Most of the time, the bed would stick about halfway through its rotation. I would be suspended at about a forty-five degree angle to the floor, which was scary. The painful part was when the apparatus got stuck; the weights that were tied to my skull for traction would swing back and forth causing my head to do the same. I was numb from the chest down, but could feel very well from the shoulders up. The swiveling of my head on my broken neck caused a throbbing as blinding as the worst migraine imaginable. Every turning session on the striker reduced me too a sobbing wreck and I was sure each time would be the one that caused my death. It was beyond excruciating and I'll never forget the sick feeling I got in my belly every time the nursing staff came into my room to turn me. This was easily the longest fourteen days of my life.

I was sustained by a phenomenon that was taking place outside my room in the lobby and on the campus of Clovis High School. I was news and everybody was talking about my injury. The hospital waiting room was full every day with my friends and some people I hardly knew. Since I was critical, I couldn't have visitors, but people came anyway just to be supportive. I can't count the letters, cards, plants, telegrams, etc. that I received from all over California. We received boxes upon boxes of mail from people who just wanted me to know I was in their prayers. If it wasn't a member of my family, a nursing student from Fresno State University would sit with me every day and read every word. There was one girl in particular named Liz who took an interest in me and checked every day to make sure I'd had my mail read. She read so many for me she felt like part of the family.

"Dear Jeff," she read on one letter in particular, "I heard about your accident at school and couldn't believe it."

Her voice was warm and soothing and I found comfort in her presence.

"I just wanted you to know how sorry I am and I am pulling for you." I remember her voice cracking as she read and I could see her tears streaming down her face. She cared, and I felt a connection to her that I would not soon forget.

The principal of our school gave updates to the student body on my progress, and it seemed like everybody was concerned. Periodically, my mom would sneak my close pals in to visit, but I was horrifying to see and it was pretty traumatic for them. Kim held vigil with my family and was in and out of my room all the time. I'm sure it was really hard, but she was being strong for me and I drew a lot of comfort from her. The only other regular visitor I was allowed was religious counsel. Hospital rules said I could pick two spiritual advisors to be at my side at any time. I was not connected to a church and didn't have any clergy that I really knew. I came to know God by hanging out at my crazy coach's house during his weekly Bible studies. Still, my first choice was my good friend Jeff. He and I had been close for about three years. He was the quarterback of our football team and since I was the center, we spent a lot of time in close proximity. He spent a lot of time looking at my rear end; so seeing me bloodied up was actually an improvement. Jeff was also a devout Christian who was always ready to talk about God. I had turned to him before, but this time was for real. He rarely left my side.

I guess I'd forgotten about the football practice incident, because I also asked Coach Bohan to be my pseudo-clergyman. I should have known, though, that it wouldn't be enough for him to hold my hand or give a shoulder on which to cry. He was a coach on a mission and I had invited him into my game. He was playing to win, but I wasn't ready to play.

My condition started to steady and I was ready to be moved to a regular room. That was a good day and meant I was finally free of the striker frame. When I was placed in a regular bed, you would have thought I'd won the lottery. My body sunk into the mattress with the same ease as when I would lay on my brother's waterbed. After the striker frame, it was soft as a feather. It wasn't exactly the Ritz-Carlton, but it was a big step up on the comfort meter. As the days passed, the goal was to be healthy enough to be transferred to a local rehabilitation hospital to begin therapy. The doctors were recommending doing my rehab in Santa Clara or Los Angeles, but I wanted my friends around during this trial. I had come from the literal darkness of ICU, but it was becoming clearer that my paralysis was not going away like the flu. I still hoped for a cure, but my timetable was moving farther away. Deep down I knew the truth, but I refused to admit that I could be in a wheelchair for life. Everything about that seemed so negative and every time I asked one of the medical experts a question about my future, the answer contained the words "no-hope" in some form or another. As I lay there in my new surroundings, it still seemed awfully dark.

I certainly had plenty of time to think. All the obvious questions ran around in my head. Will I walk? Who will hire me? Will any woman ever love me? My sixteen-year-old brain wasn't quite prepared to deal with these heavy-duty issues. Still, I found myself spending more time pondering a question that came from Coach Bohan's head and into mine. He was there every day and was always loud and upbeat as he took me through a series of scripture and motivational phrases.

One day, in about my second week in ICU, he walked in and said, "How many wins did you have today?"

I thought he was kidding because even he could see that I was in dire straits. I ignored him so he proceeded to make a list of all the things for which I could be thankful. I had a loving family, my friends were sticking by me, and I hadn't died were on the top of the chart. He didn't make me feel any better, but I was curious to why he would ask such a thing. Every day he asked me that question and I wouldn't answer. Finally, when I'd moved to my new room I had heard enough. He asked again and I countered with all the negative things I had heard.

"The doctors said that there is no-hope I'll ever walk again, no-hope I'll play football again, and no-hope I'll live a normal life again," I cried, "I don't think I have anything to be happy about."

Coach didn't even blink. He just wryly smiled and said something that I've never forgotten. "Those experts don't know Jeff Eben," he said, "and he's not gonna let the no-hopes win."

This went on day after day, week after week. It almost seemed like a game, but it wasn't funny. I didn't want to be told how lucky I was because I didn't feel very fortunate. In fact, I just wanted Coach to leave me alone.

Finally, one day when he returned, he asked again. "How many wins did you have today?"

I answered, "One. I didn't crap the bed one time."

He let out a roar that you could hear all over that hospital. We celebrated for ten minutes that I was winning. Now, I wasn't sure what I was winning, but it felt good to compete. From then on, I looked for wins every day and found them. I swallowed a piece of Jell-o, flinched my bicep, and turned without screaming (even though I was in a regular bed, I had to turn from side to side using pillows. It still hurt my neck, but it was getting manageable), anything that seemed remotely positive. With every win, Coach and anyone within earshot would celebrate as if I'd won the Super Bowl. After three weeks of this and a total of thirty-four days since I'd hit those rocks, my day was here; I was going to rehab. An ambulance came to get me and they loaded me on a stretcher. I was with Coach and some friends when the gurney was wheeled outside, my first taste of fresh air in over a month. The sun was bright and blinding, but it wasn't the only light that was shining. I left that hospital with very little, but I had a fire burning inside of me and actually was looking forward to what was ahead. As the ambulance headed downtown I celebrated my biggest win; I had found hope. I actually was beginning to believe that I could live a life that could find happiness. I'm not sure I could define the challenges that lay ahead, but I knew I wanted to see my future. I didn't know if hope would be enough but I was eager to find out.

November, 1977

*T*he moment I entered Fresno Community Hospital's Rehabilitation Unit, I knew things would be different. In the first hour, I was told I could wear my own clothes, bring my stereo, decorate my room, and have an unlimited number of visitors. I had left an environment of sickness and entered a place where all they talked about was getting well. I was being encouraged to have a life in this room, and it was amazingly refreshing. More refreshing, however, was the shower I got to take the first morning I awoke. I was wheeled on a gurney to a large, sterile room with a lot of tile. The nurse took a hand-held shower nozzle and sprayed the warm water over my head and shoulders, the only parts of my body I could feel. Having spent over a month with all the stitches in my scalp, I hadn't had my hair washed since the accident. I can only imagine the thoughts of the nursing staff outside the shower area when they heard the sounds of my groaning. The noise rivaled the best of the adult movie world, and I was not ashamed.

My mom had brought my clothes and stereo, so I was in business. She was struggling with the whole situation. Her years in the nursing profession made her vulnerable to the medical facts. She would hear the doctors talk about the limits my injury would place on my life and that would become her reality. If I talked of beating the odds, she would correct me to make sure I wouldn't get my hopes up. Mom had been through a lot with a difficult divorce and was starting to get her life back together. She had just re-married a man named Dave, and they were practically honeymooning when I got hurt. So, she was going to be sure that I didn't set myself up for any further disappointments. By now, though, I was committed to fighting everybody who doubted my ability to get my life back, so her concern didn't slow me down.

It was a little startling to have the staff dress me and discover that my clothes practically fell off of me. There was no way of hitting the scales, but I had certainly dropped in the neighborhood of fifty pounds. In fact, I bore little resemblance to the kid that went skiing on October 2nd, but I didn't spend too much time worrying about that. I was an athlete ready to compete and wanted to know the next task. Coach and I continued to count our wins, and they were plentiful in my new surroundings.

I was caught by surprise when the doctor told me it was time to learn how to sit up again. I figured they could get a chair and stick me in it, but I was painfully mistaken. I spent the month of November on something called a tilt table. Having lain flat for weeks had destroyed my equilibrium and it would be some time before I could raise my head without getting sick. It was actually dangerous because it caused a big jump in my blood pressure and I had to move slowly. Believe me when I say that I was in no hurry. The minute my head elevated caused the room to spin far worse than any cheap wine buzz I had experienced. The twice-a-day routine quickly became my least favorite part of the day. I actually knew, though, that I was going higher all the time, so I found the wins and continued on with my therapy. My short-term goal was to be able to get a special leave to attend my sister's wedding in late November. I was a groomsman, which put a serious cramp in the festivities. Once it was determined I could attend on a stretcher, we all had multiple reasons to celebrate. Coach and a few of my pals took me in a van with a nurse and I rolled down the aisle to the front of the church. I even got to go to the reception for a few minutes. I admit it wasn't the way we had planned it, but we made the most of it and I think my sister was happy. We even made the newspaper, so she was famous.

The long-term goal was to sit in a wheelchair.

The significance was two-fold: on one hand it would mean I had progressed to a point where I stopped puking every day. The other piece of importance was I could begin my physical and occupational therapy sessions. I'll never forget the roar when Coach and his wife and children turned the corner into my room and saw me sitting in my chair. We celebrated loudly and, as my room filled with the nightly crew of visitors made up of different pals from school, the party was on. The work would get harder, but that was OK. After each win, my confidence was growing. I was knocking off small tasks one at a time and was starting to believe that I could build a life and be happy. One of my favorite wins was learning how to scratch my nose. I would lay in bed for hours in the middle of the night trying to flop my arms up to my face. I was able to use my biceps to move my arms a little and wanted to get to a point where my hands reached my nose. The night I succeeded was huge. My hand was closed like a fist and it allowed me to dig my fingernails into my skin and scratch. I worked my hand back and forth for so long it drew blood. The next morning, the staff was alarmed as I had a big scab-like wound on my face that needed cleaning. It didn't matter to me, though. When Coach got there we were fired up. The "no-hopes" had lost another round.

For five months I lived in rehab. I went to therapy three times each day and was improving. I was getting movement back into my arms and a little into my wrists. I started lifting ounces of weight they would strap to my arms. It was a far cry from the Clovis High weight room where we would bench 200 pounds, but it seemed every bit as impressive. I was even re-learning how to feed myself, brush my teeth, and do daily personal care chores. The days rolled into weeks and I was flourishing in this environment. My friends had closed ranks and were a constant presence at the hospital. We were loud, obnoxious, and totally inappropriate for the setting. Thank God I had my own room, because we would have driven any roommate crazy. It was just what I needed. My friends Randy and Mike even snuck me out one night and took me to the movies. I was in my chair and they were pushing me around the hospital, which was permitted. Soon, we made it to the parking lot and they were lifting me into a car. After folding my wheelchair into the trunk, we drove off to see Burt Reynolds in "The Longest Yard." We had a great time, but I caught hell from the head nurse when I returned. I guess she wasn't amused to have a patient disappear for four hours in the night. It was entirely worth the scolding.

I made a new friend in rehab and have often wondered what the experience would have been without a guy named Flint. He was a nurse's assistant and college student. As it turned out, his father taught with mine so we had a connection. He took care of me every day for the five months I was in the unit. We would talk for hours about nothing, but we became friends. I can't believe he didn't get fired, because he spent all of his time in my room. When my friends would bring beer, he'd help them hide it. Flint was so much a part of our crowd; he even dated one of my friends who came to visit. He also connected me with life outside of the hospital. He'd talk of the antics his college pals would do and made me want to participate in some of that craziness. We'd talk music and he would make me look forward to going to concerts. Flint even arranged a pass and took me to see my brother's band play on his night off. I came to realize that Flint had a plan and it worked. He made my months in the hospital fun and showed me there were many good times to be had. I'll never forget him.

The one person I saw less and less of was Kim. She started slipping away from the regular crowd in my room at around Christmas. When she came one night and told me she was going to our school's Christmas Formal dance with some other guy, I tried to be understanding knowing you only go to high school once and she shouldn't miss out because I couldn't go. Deep down, though, I knew I was losing her. That fear was confirmed when she called a few days later to tell me she was moving on. Kim said the accident had taken its toll on her and she was ready to break things off and enjoy her days. I was crushed to some extent, but I realized that this situation was way more than she or any sixteen year old girl would sign up for in high school. I really loved her and with everything else, a broken heart wasn't what I needed, but I couldn't blame her. In fact, I'm certain if the shoe would have been on the other foot the reaction from me would have been the same. It did cement another fear I carried, however, that I'd never find a woman who would want to be with me. I had a growing confidence that I'd be physically and emotionally able to go on with life and be happy. I wondered more than once, though, if I'd have to make my way in the world without romance, which was depressing. Flint helped me get through those days, and it wasn't long before I was over my broken heart. Sure enough, the New Year came and went (including a New Year's Eve party in my room that attracted over 50 people, including, eventually, the police) and I was firmly settled into a routine designed to get strong enough to leave and get out into the real world.

My friend Dale and his family also had a tough time through my recovery. I had traveled with them during the summer and felt like they were part of my own family. Dale and I had been through thick and thin and I thought we'd be friends forever, and we were. He never said anything, but I know he had some guilt over what happened. He was the one I was with and the guy who had to pull me from the water. He heard my screams, he packed my head in towels, he lifted me into the boat with his dad and sister, and he held me for the ride to shore and in the ambulance. Though he always came around, there was a hurt in his eyes that we never talked about. At some level, there probably was some distance between us. I know this, though:

I never blamed him or his family for one second . . . ever.

Another regular part of my day was school. Our class was a close-knit bunch made closer by this ordeal. It was monumentally important to me to graduate with my friends, so I needed to stay current in my work. My health teacher was a guy named Gary Sells. He was a favorite among the students because of his Southern wit and kind heart. Mr. Sells had a thick accent and used it to draw people towards him. He was funny, yet had a deep love for God, which he unabashedly shared with his students at Bible studies. He volunteered to be my hospital teacher (I would learn later that he turned down the pay) and we went to work. He'd tape vocabulary words to my window and write papers as I dictated. I took tests orally and did well, staying on target to graduate. Most of our sessions turned into our version of Grand Ole Opry nights. He'd play his guitar and we'd sing for hours. It didn't matter who was around, Flint, my pals, Coach, or whomever. When the guitar came out, we were "pickin' and grinnin'" and everyone had to join the show.

Less enjoyable were my sessions with the rehab counselors. I guess it is part of the plan, but they were awfully negative. It seemed to me that they wanted to play it safe, so they continually filled me with how hard life would become. At some level, I guess I understand not wanting to be blamed if things don't go well, but if all I had was hope, why would they want to take that away? Continually telling me that I couldn't do things was really frustrating, and I got mad instead of sad.

One day, a team of counselors came to my bedside to discuss my education. "We want you to be able to go back to high school," one of the women exclaimed, "and we think you'll be ready by next year."

I responded, "I'm planning on going back, and I'm looking forward to being with my friends again."

This is when she dropped the bomb, "Well, you won't be able to go back to Clovis. It's not wheelchair accessible. We think you'll be better off at Hoover."

I had nothing against Hoover, but good lord! Clovis High was my home and was sustaining me throughout this time, so moving schools was . . . good lord! I was bent on proving her wrong.

The counselors also invented a program called "Meet the Pros." As I understood it, the intent of this was to ar- range monthly meetings with all of the patients in the ward and a person from the community who was living a life by which we would be inspired. I was told that we would get to talk to other disabled people who were find- ing success in the world. To this day, I don't remember one person with an uplifting story. One time, we watched a movie that rivaled any pornographic movie ever made. The film showed a paralyzed man having sex on a water- bed. The obvious point was that people in our physical condition could have a sex life. The idea was stimulating; the audience was a tad cynical.

I remember sitting there with Stan. He was in his thir- ties and the only other patient I actually hung out with. Stan had been paralyzed in a van accident, but that was only a small part of the story. As he lay under the van unable to move, battery acid dripped all over his body. He described the slow drip and it sounded like a scene from a movie. He said he put one hand over his face and one hand over his testicles, and the rest of his body was eaten up by the acid. He was badly disfigured, but I was used to him, so it was cool. As we watched the movie, the screen was filled with totally uncut sex. Stan and I, though, were whispering back and forth and trying not to laugh. Finally, he said, "Look at that wine glass on the waterbed."

I started watching the wine glass and it never moved.

43

Here was this couple thrashing around on a waterbed having wild sex, and that damn wine glass never moved or spilled. We were laughing so hard by the end the thrill of knowing that sex was possible was lost.

One community visitor was Kit, the milk guy. He had gotten out of rehab about two years earlier and came back to talk to us. He shared with us (and even brought video proof) that he had learned to open a carton of milk by himself. Other than another dude who came to tell us how hard it was to hassle with curbs and stairs, I don't remember anything else. By then, I had high hopes for my life, but they didn't come from the folks on the sixth floor, except for Flint. I wasn't the only patient in re-hab who was uninspired either. Though I lost contact with Stan, the other guys in the unit didn't fare too well. Danny, the young marine paralyzed in a car crash, died a few years later from pneumonia, I heard. The same with Kelly, another car crash victim who was sixteen like me. Luther and Tush (short for something, I don't know) both were in rehab for something secretive, though I know it involved police. Both have passed away. As far as I know, I'm the only one who survived beyond five years. Whatever the medical reason for their death, I knew in the hospital that they all had lost their will. So, the pros weren't all that inspiring.

What occurred during my six-month stay in the hospital is hard to describe. Coach was there every day and we continued to pile up daily victories. He had me convinced that I was a participant in this long football season where every day was a new opponent. I was also learning that losing in this game was not an option and I was willing to fight like hell. My therapies were like practice and I treated them as such. I screamed and yelled like a wild man and wanted to do all the things the doctors told me weren't possible. I was getting more strength and move-ment in my arms and started pushing my chair to the gym each day. It all seemed very normal and even fun.

44

My friends, family, and I were daily fixtures at the hospital, and it became easy to be a part of that culture. I was becoming "institutionalized."

Luckily, I was able to eventually get passes to go home. I spent a day at school where I was treated like a hero. This was a big moment in my emotional recovery. I had a few deep fears, and the reaction to me from my peers was at the top of the list. I'm not sure this is even rational, but I had been one of the guys. I fit in and belonged to a couple of different groups on campus. I was on the football team and in student leadership. I was happy in both places and felt like I was part of both groups. I was terrified of being ostracized or forgotten. The thought of being the little handicapped boy that everyone stared at was horrifying to me and fed a sense of insecurity I had to get over. The love I felt that day bolstered my desire to return to my life. The peace I got from that visit was huge.

My house was a steady stream of visitors who weren't in my normal circle, so it was good to re-connect with acquaintances and family friends. After one of the weekend visits, I knew it was time to come home. I missed my old life and knew if I didn't get back to it, I'd get too comfortable and the world would move on without me. It was mid-April when I asked my doctor when I would be released. I was stunned when he told me I could check out in the coming weekend. I reacted excitedly and though our house wasn't ready, we made plans to leave the comforts of rehab. I have often wondered how long I would have stayed in the hospital if I didn't ask to leave. I never went back and questioned my doctor, but I always thought he was waiting for me to be ready. Guess I'll never know.

I continued to go to therapy until the end. I was leaving on a Saturday morning, but I took my full complement of sessions. On my last Thursday, something interesting happened. I was pushing myself back to my room and had wandered into a hallway that wasn't on my normal route. There was a beautiful young nurse there, and she surprised me by knowing my name. She did look familiar and I realized it was Liz, the student nurse from the Intensive Care Unit at the other hospital. She was the one who would read to me and I immediately felt a soft spot for her in my heart. We exchanged small talk and I discovered that she graduated and was working at this hospital as a floor nurse. We laughed as I told her I was leaving in a couple of days and we'd missed our time to visit. She did, however, offer to come by when she got off at about midnight and I was thrilled.

The door cracked open right on time and Liz came in. It was very quiet and we had to whisper, but we talked for a couple of hours. Our conversation went from my accident to dating, the whole range of small talk. She was twenty-three and I was sixteen, but I was completely attracted to her. I even asked her if she would date someone my age and was only mildly disappointed when she said she wouldn't. Liz knelt down to kiss me goodbye and I decided to go for it. She pulled away and said, "No," but it wasn't very convincing. She left and I lay in my bed wondering what had just happened. Surprisingly, I wasn't that embarrassed. I had felt some passion on her end and was pretty excited.

I was not surprised when my door opened at midnight the next evening, my last night in the rehab hospital. When Liz had left the night before, we had connected and I thought about her all day. Apparently, she felt the same and was standing in the dim light of my room long after everyone on my floor had gone to sleep. She said she had thought about my question and wanted to change her answer. She said she would go out with a sixteen year old, and that person would be me. We kissed for a long time and she had to go. I never saw her again, but she gave me quite a gift in helping ease another of my greatest fears.

It was time to go home. I was proud of the fact that I'd come through an incredibly difficult and frightening event and maintained a good attitude and a sense of humor. It hit me on Sunday night when I was on my couch. When I had come home before, I had to be back at the hospital by the evening. This time, dusk came and went and I was home for good. I had faced the biggest challenge I could have ever imagined and I won. Unfortunately, the game was just starting and I had no idea what would come next.

April, 1978

I looked forward to going back to my high school from the moment I returned. I had to make some adjustments, though, that took a little time. The first one was that we had moved when I was in the hospital. When my parents divorced when I was twelve, we lived in an upscale community in the Los Angeles area called La Canada. We had moved from our Fresno home so my father could become the head football coach at the high school. His teams did poorly and he was replaced after two years and kept walking right out of our lives. With my older brother, Jon, and Suzi grown and out of the house, my mom took my brother Scott and me back to Fresno. We had little money and lived in a mobile home in a Fresno area trailer park for four years. When my mother re-married when I was fourteen, things got better. In a year, we were building a house and could put the trailer park days behind us. Our new house was completed while I was in rehab, so I came home to all new surroundings. The only bad thing was that to accommodate the wheelchair, we needed major re-modeling, which was unfinished when I got home for good. We converted a couch in the living room and I made camp there until my new room was complete.

My good friend Scott and his family took good care of us. Scott's dad was a very successful builder who had created a hugely profitable company by building apartment complexes and office buildings. My friend was one of those guys who had everything you'd ever want but you'd never know it. He was quiet and as unassuming as it gets. In fact, Scott was sometimes on the outside of our inner circle. He worked so much, he never got to hang out. One night during the end of my stay in the hospital, he and his dad showed up at our new home. They said they were concerned about the accessibility of the house and offered to help re-model. Big Scott's (the dad) only warning was that if he did the work, it would not be a sterile, hospital-type room. He wanted it to be cool and a place my friends could come and hang.

For about a month, construction crews lived at our place. As I lay on the couch, we were besieged with framers, plumbers, and electricians who transformed two small bedrooms into one big teenager's quarters equipped with a bathroom, alarm system, stereo, and remote control television. I got to choose the carpet and wallpaper and picked a tasteful pattern that included nude women covering every inch of the design. Honestly, you can't show that to a red-blooded teenaged boy and not expect him to select the girls. Finally, the room was ready and after weeks on the couch, I moved in. Not surprisingly, we never received the bill for that project.

Another adjustment was a little more personal. My new life required some daily routines that left me with virtually no privacy. My mom or another member of my family had to dress and undress me in the morning and evening. Having everybody see me naked was bad, but I got over it fairly soon. That wasn't the worst part, though. Every four hours I had to drain my bladder through a process called intermittent catheterization. Any shame I had was put to rest early on because there was no choice but to expose myself. The process involved inserting a tube through the hole on the tip of the organ you'd least like to have a tube inserted. Though I couldn't feel it, I could see it and it looked painful. As days went by, every member of my family and many of my friends learned how to catheterize me. Actually, the more people who knew the procedure helped me increase my independence and made returning to school easier, but I had to get through the embarrassment. After awhile, it seemed everyone in Clovis had seen me with my pants down.

The only obstacle standing between school and me was transportation. We didn't have a van at all, let alone one with a lift. My mother worked with the school district to provide some sort of accessible bussing. After some effort, the school acquired the services of a bus that catered to the disabled. Some adjustments were made in my class schedule so all of my courses were downstairs and I was ready. I had received an electric wheelchair after a couple of weeks at home. The intent was to allow me to make my way around the large campus. The freedom that it gave me should be what is advertised on the flyer. I could move around the house as I pleased and not have to be pushed. I could walk around the block at my leisure and enjoy the fresh air. It wasn't as good as getting the use of my legs back, but it was close. Around the first of May, and after seven months of being away, I returned to Clovis High School. I remembered the no-hope crew that had told me I wouldn't be able to return to my school because it wasn't wheelchair accessible and it made me smile. I was quickly learning that my destiny was to be decided by me, and Coach Bohan and I celebrated another win.

The first day was exciting and nerve wracking. I was a different guy than the person who left there in October, another lifetime ago. I looked different, felt different, and was scared of the reaction from my peers. As I waited for my bus to pull up outside my house, I got cold feet. Before I could change my mind, though, the bus arrived and a driver got out to take me to school. He hit a button that swung open the back door. Another button brought a large lift down to the ground. I wheeled around and backed onto the platform. The driver started to raise me up and I realized it was time to make it in the world on my own. No more nurses, no mother waiting on me. I was headed out and my survival depended on my ability to conquer the public's misconception of people in wheelchairs. As the door closed on my mom and stepfather, I was determined to fit in and be as able as anyone else. I decided to not acknowledge any difference and go about my day, as if I'd never left.

As the bus pulled away from my house, it was strangely silent. There were about four other people on the bus, all adults. What struck me as odd was only one other person was in a wheelchair, the rest were able-bodied and I couldn't figure out why they were traveling with me. The driver made his way down a bumpy road and was going way too fast when he made a quick turn. The sway in the back was severe and the lady in the wheelchair fell over. She let out a scream that I'll never forget and pandemonium broke out. As our guy pulled over, the sobbing was loud and I realized that I was in a different world. Besides being in a chair, this poor gal on the floor was severely mentally retarded and was crying like an infant. It was at that moment that I understood why the other riders were there. They, too, had the mental capacity of young children and were frightened by what had occurred. These folks began crying, jumping up and down in their seats, and yelling words that were unintelligible. The noise was deafening and I closed my eyes thinking I was having another bad dream. The driver was quite amused by it all and lifted the girl and her chair right side up. The damage was done, though, and I rode the longest fifteen-mile bus ride of my life in the midst of these screaming, hysterical adults who could not help themselves.

I'm embarrassed to admit that I was totally undone by that experience. I got to school and went immediately to the office and announced that I'd never ride that bus again. My doubts about my new existence were strong enough without being made to ride on a bus where everyone is developmentally delayed. I wanted to be "normal" and my immature brain told me that bus made me look pathetic. I told my friend Ray about the trip and he offered me a ride home, which I accepted. The school day was a blur, but I was welcomed with open arms. After school, I met Ray and he lifted me in his arms and put me in his Buick Regal. After careful planning, he somehow managed to lift my two hundred pound chair into his trunk and we drove home with the trunk wide open. We reversed the process and went into the house with my first day in the bag. As I told my mom of the morning's adventure, I made it clear I wasn't getting on that bus again. We had no answer for how I'd get to school, though, and I thought for a second my return to Clovis High would last all of one day. As soon as the doubt came into my mind, Ray spoke up and volunteered to transport me to and from school every day. Ray was a gifted athlete, an all-everything defensive back in football and a standout in track and field. Even with his skills, the lifting we had just completed was hard, but he was sincere and assured us it would be no problem. We only had about six weeks left in our junior year and we told him if he could get us through this period of uncertainty, we'd have a permanent solution for our senior year. Ray laughed and told us that HE was the permanent solution and would work for food every day until we graduated. From that day forward, I never worried about a ride again, and my mother kept him fed. I'm still not sure who got the best end of that deal, but Ray became a regular part of the family.

That first day on campus was a blur. All eyes were on me all day, but they were looks of pride and compassion, not weirdness. My classmates made me feel welcome and I must've said hello to all three thousand students that day. The one class that stood out that day was my sixth period science class. Mr. Jarl was the teacher and I had maybe said two words to him in my years at school. I didn't know him at all. He was tall, blonde, and worked on the ski patrol, but that was all I knew. I sat against the wall behind a row of chairs and didn't say anything during the fifty minutes. It was April and the class was in the middle of the semester so I was coming into a conversation that was far along. So I sat there and drifted off.

At the end of the period, he asked if I'd stay to talk. After everyone left, he said something about covering topics in class about the body and if anything bothered me I could say something and he'd excuse me. I didn't feel that was necessary, but it was a nice gesture and I knew he was genuinely reaching out. Then he said something I never forgot.

"I just want you to know that you've handled this situation and yourself very well."

That was it. I don't know why that meant so much, but I never forgot it. I think he made me feel strong and I needed to be strong. I was trying hard to make my life work and his small comment validated me. My psyche was working overtime, and I hung to words and phrases and found profound meaning in words like "How many wins . . ." and "no-hopes." I was searching for anything that would make my new life OK, and he gave me something. I was really proud.

In truth, I'm pretty sure I didn't do a lot of good to the world of academia between the time I returned to school and summer vacation. I learned a few things about my new body that were troubling. I noticed if it got hot, which Fresno does quite well, my body would react. I discovered that my sweat glands were paralyzed and didn't work when I heated up. There were days at school I had to leave because my body temperature rose to a point where I'd start to pass out. If I didn't cool down, I'd risk a stroke. I also discovered that even though I was catheterized every four hours, occasionally I would look down and notice that I had wet my pants, not a proud moment for a teenage boy trying to be a man.

Most of that six-week period, though, taught me how lucky I was to be surrounded by the people in my community. The novelty of my return wore off quickly and every day became business as usual. I had my circle of friends and we had our territory. They took turns taking care of my bathroom needs and most of the guys had classes with me in case of an emergency. We just hung out and visited every day as usual. The only big change was every student on campus knew my name so I never went more than a few yards without stopping to say hello to someone. If we were doing our thing in the bathroom, people just walked around us and made conversation like nothing was amiss. It was pretty nice to know I was being allowed to be a normal part of the culture by my peers. Even more, it was clear they were glad I was back and wanted me to succeed.

The adults on campus and in town went out of their way to be supportive. Teachers moved their rooms so I could attend their classes easier. There was no accommodation that wasn't made for my work. If I needed an aide to help write, I got one. If I needed to take a test orally, it happened. Our principal was a guy named William J. Contente, and he stayed connected to me and my family throughout the ordeal. He was tireless and had a bond with his students; we loved him. He made sure everything was right and made personal contact on a daily basis. When I was in rehab, he even arranged a telephone hook-up from my hospital room to our gym where we were having a pep rally. To hear three thousand people cheering for me was beyond description, but those were the types of gestures made for me. Even though I knew I was blessed by the people in my life, nothing could have prepared me for what was about to transpire.

One day in the middle of May, I was summoned to the principal's office. Mr. Contente usually saw me out on campus, but it wasn't too far-fetched for him to call me in, so I wasn't alarmed. When I got there, we made some small talk before he told me he had a plan on which he was working. Mr. C. (he liked to call himself that even though we never used it) was a student-centered administrator. A talented musician, he had been the band director before entering administration. From time to time, he'd serenade us with his trumpet and it was pretty darned good. He took over our school when my class entered as freshmen, so he always said we were special and we bought it hook, line, and sinker. He was very cool, too. He dressed beautifully, all the way down to his white shoes that were stylish in the 1970's. Mr. Contente had a trademark, though, and that was his hair. It was pure white and he grew it long on one side so he could comb it around to cover his bald spot. The kicker was, he was totally open about it and even got into the dunk tank so his secret was visible to everyone at school. That kind of thing made him more popular with the students and it felt like he was our friend.

Mr. C. knew my family didn't have a lot of money and we had all we could handle to stay afloat. He told me he was concerned about my future and my ability to be independent. He thought a van with a lift would help and thought I'd even be able to drive, something I hadn't yet considered. I knew nothing about the cost or process involved, but before I could even ask a question, he said he wanted to have our school and community raise some twenty-five thousand dollars to go toward the purchase of this vehicle. When I left his office, he had declared May 19th as Jeff Eben Day at school. It seemed like only hours before the city council in Clovis and Fresno made the same declaration. Soon, I would hear from our congressman, state assemblyman, and then Governor Jerry Brown proclaiming this day in my honor in the State of California. I was very grateful but pretty embarrassed. The train had left the station, though, and there wasn't much I could do about it. As it turned out, my mom had talked to Mr. C. and he knew the financial bind we were in. I also learned that the mom of my friend, Criss, worked in the Democratic Party and got a hold of Governor Brown's staff who put things together for me. I was well cared for.

The next day, Mr. Contente called the students to the gym for an assembly. He pulled me out on the floor in front of my classmates and rallied them to help. The bottom line was, on the evening of the 19th, which was about a week away, we would have a large celebration in the gym. The choir would sing, the band would play, and individuals from all over would come to speak or sing. What he asked of the kids was to show up with names and pledges of people who would donate to the cause. He asked clubs and organizations to work on projects to raise money and dismissed the students back to class. I was mortified, but the students gave a loud ovation and actually went to work. For the next several days, my face was everywhere. This event drew coverage from every television station and the local newspapers. My friends put posters up all over the school and town.

May 19th couldn't come fast enough as I cringed at the thought of people giving me money. The night arrived, though, and it was beyond successful. Everyone I'd ever heard of showed up to be a part of the night. Local merchants brought money, and the churches, government agencies, and community members seemed to all participate. The lion's share of the work, though, was done by our students. They went door to door, washed cars, held dances, and even donated a huge portion of the profit from the Junior/Senior Prom to this event. In a touch of irony, that particular check was presented during the evening by my former sweetheart Kim, who had chaired the Prom. She said some really nice things, but when I went up there, we didn't speak. She kissed me on the cheek and I went back to my friends. As quickly as that interaction passed, I think it signaled the end of any tension, and Kim and I became friends again. It was a little awkward for me, but my pals found great humor in the moment. When the fundraising portion of the night ended, they had raised over twenty grand for my van. I was just speechless, but I was pretty relieved it was over. The gym was packed, but the adults were cleared and we got to have a dance for a couple of hours and had a great time.

As surprised as I was at the success of the event, I was happier and more surprised by something else that happened that night. There was a girl named Michelle there who I had actually dated a year and a half earlier. She was a beautiful girl with golden brown hair that was very shiny because she spent a lot of time in the pool. Michelle was actually a champion swimmer, a cheerleader, and a girl who was really involved in school. Even though our fifteen-year-old romance didn't last, we were friends and ran around in the same crowd. I was scared of the whole girl thing and hadn't quite recovered from having my heart broken. Mostly, though, I was unsure of myself and was not remotely interested in plunging into that scene . . . or so I thought.

I found myself dancing with Michelle over and over again. There was no wheelchair dance model, so I just went out and moved my arms as much as possible to the music. I'm sure it was awful, but nobody had the heart to tell me that on my own day. I figured out the slow songs a little easier and would just have my partner sit on my lap, arms around my neck, as I'd spin my chair in a circle. I liked the slow songs, but noticed every time the tempo decreased, I was looking for Michelle. To my surprise, I didn't have to look very hard after awhile and soon she just stayed on my lap for the rest of the night.

Sure enough, during one of the slow songs, our lips locked and we stayed that way for awhile. I'm not sure if it was her kiss or the fact that I was kissing someone that made me almost crawl out of my skin. After the shock wore off I realized it was her and I was very thrilled. The dance was in its last thirty minutes and when the song ended, I knew I was done dancing and wanted to lose myself for the evening with her. We went outside to be alone and found a dark corner outside of the gym. We rarely spoke, but she communicated beautifully. I don't remember how long we were out there, but I remember what happened when we left. As I kissed her goodnight, I was really feeling it and I blurted out, "I hope this isn't a one-night thing."

Then she answered, "So do I." Needless to say, I went home a pretty happy camper. I thought about her all weekend and when I got to school, she was waiting for me. Immediately, we were a couple and I couldn't have been happier. My friends included her in all of our week-end foolishness, and by the time the school year faded into summer, we were very close. All I knew was that May 19th was the day that my friends and neighbors gave me a gift of love that took years for me to understand. The tangible reward was a van, for gosh sakes. The real reward, however, was the peace and strength I felt knowing that I was surrounded by a group of people who would give so much of themselves. I'm pretty sure, though, that all of that was the second best thing that happened to me that night. I had a girlfriend and that did more for my psyche at that point than the van. Fortunately, I didn't have to choose and enjoyed both tremendously.

August, 1978

*T*here are a lot of milestones in life and a senior
year in high school ranks right up with the best of them.
My house was the summer gathering spot for my circle of
friends and our girlfriends, and we counted the days until
school started when we took our rightful spot at the top of
the power structure. The group effort of nursing me back
to health had drawn us unusually close and we spent
every day together in one way or another. As excited as I
was for the upcoming year and even proud of how far I'd
progressed with my attitude in tact, August came and the
reality of my life was bittersweet at best. You see, I grew
up dreaming not of graduation. That was a given. For
me, it was all about playing for a Valley football championship (that eluded my father and brothers), earning
all-conference honors, and playing in the annual City/
County All Star Game. With our team ranked among the
top two or three in our section, all of these dreams were
reasonable, but fate intervened and when training camp
started two weeks before school opened, I was on the
sidelines for the first time since I donned pads in the fifth
grade. I put on a brave face, but the pain I felt was unbearable and haunts me to this day. It sounds silly, but I
had waited for this moment my entire life. I'd watched so
many high school games as a child, being out on the field
on a Friday night was larger than life . . . and I missed
it. I will go to my grave just wishing I could have had one
game as a senior . . . just one. This was the place in my
life where things changed, so I think that is why I feel so
unfulfilled over football. I was so close and didn't get to
finish the deal.

Coach Bohan made me his assistant and even assigned
me a job as the coach of the centers, so it wasn't totally
ceremonial. We had two at that position, both pretty good

pals of mine. Eddie was the starter and did a great job. I had been projected as the guy for this year, so when I went down, the coaching staff used the off-season to move him from the defense to take my place. We were close and Eddie listened to me, so I felt surprisingly useful. The other center was a guy named Ron who had played behind me on the freshman and junior varsity teams so, even though we ran in different circles, our relationship was solid and he also let me coach him. (It should be noted that Eddie became all-everything and earned a football scholarship. Ron went on to win the California Lottery and became an instant millionaire, so my work was clearly solid.) The season was off and running and I tried to be excited and enjoy myself. Luckily, we started winning and I found joy in the success.

School opened and that was much easier. Most of my requirements were out of the way, so I did things that I thought would be fun. I was very musical so I sang in the choir and loved it. I also joined the broadcasting program and worked my way up to be the news anchor for our weekly television show that was shown in our community every Saturday night. The school staff let me do the morning announcements so the student body had to start every day by hearing my voice. I was definitely overexposed, but nobody seemed to mind. Coach even assigned me to be his assistant during one period of each day and we would report to the weight room where he put me through workouts that were more rigorous than the football players went through. We were quite a pair and my high school career is defined by that relationship as much as anything else.

As the school year progressed, my relationship with Michelle became very close. We were in love. Our football team had lost one game, but we were cruising through the year and were poised to play for the league title and were all but assured of making the Valley playoffs as we got to our last league game. The guys on the team were

Big Men on Campus and in town, and no one was more recognizable than me. As expected, as seniors we had the run of the school, so we were having a ball. Under the circumstances, the Class of 1979 at Clovis High had nothing to complain about. For me, though, it was still bittersweet.

As good as I tried to make it, I missed playing ball and felt really isolated on Friday nights. I could not have asked for anyone to do more to make me feel included, but it wasn't the same. I tried hard through the season to be happy, but it was hard to watch everybody else get to do something that I loved so much. The games were almost surreal and I couldn't quite get a grasp on the fact that I was really sitting on the sidelines. I was waiting for the alarm to go off and end this dream, but it didn't. Strangely enough, I only felt that way on Friday nights.

I'll never forget the last game of the year. It is still considered one of the best high school football games ever played in our area and decided our league's playoff birth. We came back from way behind to have a chance to win. Like in a cheesy sports flick, we threw a pass in the end zone as time ran out, and our guy caught it. I rolled out with the rest of my teammates and celebrated a miraculous finish. I was genuinely excited, but we missed the ensuing extra point and lost. Everyone sat there stunned as our season was over. I did feel bad for my friends because they wanted to go the playoffs and were so close. The truth was, though, I was relieved the season was over. From that night on, I moved past football and wouldn't look back for many years. Unfortunately, things would get worse before they got better.

Around the same time, my relationship with Michelle took an unexpected turn for the worse. Her mother was not at all pleased with our relationship. She didn't see any reason for her daughter to spend time with a guy in a wheelchair and started to keep us apart. This was my first bout with any form of discrimination and it got harder and harder to take. To her credit, Michelle said she loved me and didn't care and was even willing to continue to defy her mom. I couldn't understand, though. After all I'd endured I felt like I deserved to be happy. By now I was seventeen and figured I was old enough not to have to lie and sneak to spend time with someone I loved. Proving my immaturity, though, I gave Michelle an ultimatum. She was to convince her mom that we could have an open relationship or we were through . . . the next day we were through.

Christmas break was a week away and life was slowly getting back to normal, although I still had heartache. Randy, Eddie, and I were nominated for Christmas Formal King, so we all made plans to go together and I asked my good friend Catherine to be my date. The dance was Saturday as we headed into the two-week Christmas vacation, so it seemed like a good night to blow off some steam left over from football championships and loves lost. We actually were supposed to go back to school for three days the week after the formal, but we had no intention of returning. For us, the dance marked vacation, and we were ready.

By Friday of that week a flu epidemic hit our school and we had almost one-third of our students absent. My buddies and I had escaped it and we were happy to get out of there. The only exception was Dale. By that afternoon, we had gathered in the locker room to make our plans for the night, and he was a mess. Dale was one of the top wrestlers in the state and as soon as football ended, he started cutting weight for his division. He was very small anyway and to try and lose weight seemed crazy, but he did it every year so it was nothing new. He was a year older than us and was the first to drive, turn eighteen, everything. Dale was the leader in our circle and was with me when I got hurt, so he was special. As sick as he was in that locker room, though, we were worried. We even had someone drive him home on Friday and help him get to bed. We all ended up going home and figured we'd live it up at the Formal.

Saturday started out like any other day except we had big plans that night. Jeff had come by to hang out for awhile and we were in my room passing time until we needed to get ready. For one of the very few times since my accident, my dad was at the house talking to my mom. Their divorce was bitter, so the two of them in the same room was news, but it wouldn't come close to being the news of the day. The phone rang about eleven in the morning and Jeff answered. I saw the expression on his face and knew something was wrong. He put the phone down and muttered that Dale had gone into cardiac arrest at his house and was rushed to the hospital. Dale's dad owned a service station and Jeff worked there so he called to see if anyone knew anything. I don't remember what he found out, but he tore out and said he'd call me when he heard anything. After sitting in silence for awhile, I went out and told my folks what happened. We waited for what seemed like an eternity but heard nothing.

At about one that afternoon, Coach Bohan called with news. He had spoken with the same hospital to which Dale had accompanied me in the minutes after my accident one year earlier. Officials there confirmed that our friend had died of a bleeding ulcer that morning. He had lost too much weight too quickly and it literally ate a hole in his stomach. Dale had tried to cut his weight from one hundred fifty pounds to one hundred twelve pounds and his body didn't adjust. Just as I hung up, my friend Criss showed up with a big smile as usual. He and Dale were pals and also neighbors, even having identical gold Trans-Ams, which we all thought was a riot. There was nothing funny today and as I broke the news to Criss, he said nothing, walked out the door and drove off. The news started to spread and our house became the center of a crowd of young people in various stages of shock.

There was a poster that hung in my room before, during, and after my accident. It showed five young high school boys in the prime of their lives. It was taken in the spring of 1977 at a school dance where we were acting goofy and had our picture taken as a group. There actually were about seven or eight of us in our circle, but only five had attended this dance and took the photograph. When I was in the hospital, the guys blew it up into a poster that adorned the wall of my rehab room and then in my home. To look at that picture in December of 1978 and realize that one of those young men was dead and another paralyzed for life in separate incidents was a lot to fathom.

Dale's funeral was poignant. The church was overflowing and the guys in the group all served as pallbearers even though I couldn't carry the casket. We sat together, hand in hand, but spoke very little. It was hard to imagine being put through any more difficult life lessons than our bunch of friends had to endure in that year or so. We gripped each other a little tighter and it seemed like we were clinging for dear life. We looked at each other as if to wonder what or who would be next. All I knew is that we had seen our share of pain and we all limped off to Christmas with broken hearts. We would never forget our friend or these powerful friendships that became very important during this time in our young lives.

We came back to school and, as young people do, we moved forward. The senior thing had lost its luster when Dale left us, but we finished the year. It was time to start thinking about the future, but we were all pretty attached, so leaving wasn't that appealing. Randy, Jeff, and I sort of separated from the others, though we all stayed close. A new friend to our group named Sal hung with us and we were looking at college. Criss and Scott were both from successful family-owned businesses, so their futures were secure. Ray was planning on continuing to play football, so we were going in a few different directions. Truth was, life had given us an education and in the last few months of our senior year, we weren't particularly interested in what school had to offer. We even drifted away from Coach, though we still revered him.

About the only joy we derived in our last few months was figuring out how many ways we could beat the system. It started simply and grew into grand stunts. Being a good student proved useful to my partners-in-crime. I would take my tests in class orally, usually right outside the door. As I gave my answers, I spoke loudly enough so my friends who had moved close to the door could hear. I'm proud to say I helped a few struggling seniors graduate who might not otherwise have been able to attend the ceremony in June.

More fun was the ability to leave school at will when the weather warmed up. All it would take is my feigning heat related weakness and we were home free. Usually that meant a rendezvous for anyone who was interested at our little spot near the Kings River. We would drink beer, barbecue, and hang together in an unspoken fear of our friendships coming to an end. Some days there were five of us at the river, other days we'd have a crowd of twenty. Our river parties had guys and girls flittering their final days together away with no apparent purpose. It was awesome.

Probably my personal crowning glory came on our last news broadcast of the year. I had been promising something big on the air for weeks. It was finally time to deliver. We taped on Friday and the show ran Saturday, so we had time to edit and change things, making this little stunt possible. One of the other anchors introduced me as out on a live shot and the director cut to me out in front of the school. I was wearing a helmet and we had parked two trucks facing each other with a wooden ramp going up one side and another ramp coming down on the other side. I explained that as a gift to my friends for all their support, I wanted to jump the two trucks in my wheelchair ala Evil Kneivel. I took a couple runs at the ramp and pronounced myself ready with the disclaimer "Please don't try this at home." I headed full speed toward the ramp and my chair climbed toward the truck. As I passed the midpoint of the ramp, the director cut the shot and announced that technical difficulties had arisen. I carefully backed down the ramp and moved to the other side of the set. I backed up on the ramp to give the appearance that I had made the jump and was descending the second board. I jostled myself to make it look like a rough landing and the spot was finished. When our student crew put it all together, it was perfect and looked almost real. If it wasn't so silly, it almost could have appeared believable. A bunch of us gathered at my house to watch it the next night on television. It came off pretty well and we were quite pleased with ourselves. As soon as the segment went off and we were reveling in our stupidity, the phone rang. An adult from our community called to tell me he was watching and was amazed at my bravery. He even went on to say his television went out right before I went airborne, but he was glad to see that I'd made it safely. And he was serious! I was so proud.

Much of our time during the last couple of weeks of school was spent making fools of ourselves. We didn't mind, though. Frankly, the world's opinion of us was irrelevant and we felt like we'd earned some time to let our hair down. Those days were the safest of my life and the people in my memory from those times are the best friends I'd ever know. In its own way, that was a magical time and as graduation approached, I could reflect on my high school experience as a time where I learned the tools to overcome my life's adversity. There was no doubt that our senior class walked into our beautiful football stadium on the evening of our commencement knowing, if nothing else, we had grown up. It wasn't easy, but it was real and we were better for the experience.

The wind blew hard as I sat in my cap and gown in front of the thousands of people gathered for the ceremony. My mind wandered and I missed Dale. In fact, our class lost five students to death during our four years, so virtually every graduate had their own Dale. Rather than be sad, I tried to find perspective, and there was plenty. I tried to process what I had learned in my four years, and I realized that I was coming away with a formula for life: Coach Bohan had shown me that in our darkest moment there was still hope that could be found by simply counting our wins. My circle of friends taught me a lesson in unconditional love that I'll never forget. On that graduation platform that night, I got misty-eyed knowing I had been blessed with gifts that some people never receive. Shoot, I even got the taste of being in love, which made me hungry for more. In fact, I was even willing to risk getting my heart broken again to find someone to love. In all the craziness, I left my high school with few regrets, but plenty of questions. The most important question was, "Did I have the tools and fortitude necessary to build a life for myself away from the comfortable surroundings of high school?" Hope and love are great, but I wondered more than once if they were enough.

II

Applying the Power of Hope and Love Provided my Life Meaning and Direction.

August, 1979

And this is where my story begins. You see, from the moment I landed in the hospital, I was swamped with stories of the human spirit. Well meaning friends, acquaintances, and folks I'd never met brought me articles and books of various people in the world who had encountered serious injuries in their lives and survived.

Once I was able to have visitors, I started to hear the stories of accident victims who faced similar challenges and lived to tell about them. The first one I heard was the story of Jill Kinmont. Rita, a family friend, came to see me and had a book in her hands called The Other Side of the Mountain. Miss Kinmont was a famous skier who broke her neck and became paralyzed. There was a movie made from her book, and she had become quite a household name. Her story told of losing her fiancé after her accident but finding enough strength to re-build her life. She became a teacher up in an area near Mammoth, California and was living a full, happy life. Rita read parts of it to me, but I tuned her out. I had nothing against Jill, but it didn't have anything to do with me since there was no way I was going to be paralyzed. Frankly, I felt the same when someone else brought me the book Joni, an autobiography by a gal named Joni Erickson that told a similar story of successfully starting over after being paralyzed. Again, it wasn't me.

One night, though, my phone rang. My coach happened to be there, picked up the phone and placed it to my ear. "Jeff," the caller said, "this is Merrill Womach."
I was stunned. Mr. Womach was a man who had his face burned off in a fire. I had heard his story through our Fellowship of Christian Athletes' group before I had gotten hurt. Coach Bohan used to play his tapes and had

shown us a movie of his recovery. I remember being awed by how happy he seemed, even though he was totally disfigured. He told of singing this little song when the doctors were wheeling him down to the operating room for surgery immediately after his accident. I remembered thinking he was the most courageous person I'd ever seen and his song made a lasting impression on me. In fact, when I was being wheeled down to surgery in the days immediately after my accident, his was the voice I heard in my head. I began to copy his behavior as I got closer to the operating room and serenaded the surgical team with his song, "I was Happy Before, I'll be Happy Again." So, to hear his voice on the phone was amazing.

I don't remember much of what he said, but the tone of his voice will never leave me. He was loud and strong, and I vividly recall flinching at his volume. It's hard to describe, but he was the happiest sounding man I'd ever heard on the phone. There was almost a song-like quality in his voice; a deep baritone that belonged in a barbershop quartet. He laughed constantly and reminded me when he hung up that I would be OK. I believed him and, for the first time, was ready to listen to the stories of others.

I was struck by the common themes of active person, devastating injury, thoughts of death, and ultimately acceptance. In some of these cases, movies were made as a testimony to the strength of the human spirit and the power of a person's capacity to overcome. Like many others, I was moved by a few of the tales and found solace in the message that it was possible to live through trauma and emerge with a level of happiness and peace.

My problem after my high school graduation was simple but profound: I accomplished the mission of survival and was plenty happy. I had come through my significant challenge with a good attitude and a confidence in my own resolve. I had done so well that my school and community held a day in my honor and heard words like "hero" and "courageous" frequently. The people in my life had fallen into a trap where I was being rewarded on a regular basis for the simple fact that I was a survivor. As nice as it was, graduation marked the end of that period of my life. The balloons had popped, the confetti was swept up, and the cheering had stopped. Life had officially turned a corner and despite all the attention, I was still an eighteen-year-old kid with my whole life ahead of me. I didn't have much of a plan, nor was I really serious about anything. During that first summer after high school, though, I knew I hadn't accomplished anything and needed to start adulthood. College seemed the logical place to start. College by the beach, however, seemed brilliant.

To show how little thought I had put into the college selection process, however, consider that I had decided based on my high school experiences on television that broadcasting was my life's passion and applied to Cal Poly San Luis Obispo. I was accepted into the School of Speech and Communication and at my orientation in September, I learned that broadcasting had nothing to do with speech and communications and I was in the wrong department. That wouldn't have been a big deal as I could transfer to the right area by just moving my paper work. The problem came when I found out that Cal Poly didn't even have a broadcasting department. Here I had scholarship money, student loans, and other financial aid from a school that didn't even offer what I wanted. Further, I had already moved into my off campus dorm with Randy and Sal, my close pals who shared my enthusiasm for a beach-enhanced education. So, I pretended like I knew this information all along and enrolled in general education courses. It was going to be fine. We were at the beach, my sister had started her family and lived close by, my brother Jon's band was famous in the Central Coast area, and my father's home was within ten miles. I was clueless about living on my own, but I acted like I had it under control.

If there was any doubt in my mind that I had made the right decision to come to San Luis Obispo (SLO), it was erased during the first week. The parties were endless and, everywhere we turned, the beer was free and plentiful. In a strange twist of fate, I had an unplanned reunion with a group of friends from my elementary and junior high school years spent in La Canada. Our family had only lived in the Los Angeles area for four years, but I had made some friends there and had been sad to leave them. As much as I tried to keep in touch, I had lost contact with many of the people from that period of my life. There had been a couple of folks with whom I kept up, and I received some beautiful cards and letters from some familiar names from that community. Mostly, though, La Canada was a pleasant memory until we arrived at college.

Sal had moved to the beach about a month prior to Randy and me. He was attending Cuesta Junior College, which was near Cal Poly. He was living by himself and had made a few friends when he met two girls named Moody Cabanillas and Kathy Rhoades on campus. After small talk, Sal talked about being from Fresno, and they remembered that I had moved there. They asked the needle in a haystack question of whether Sal knew me, and he told them of our friendship and that I was coming soon. Both girls had been pretty good friends of mine in seventh grade, so when Sal called to tell me the news, I was pretty thrilled. At least I knew that the world was smaller than I realized. Stranger still, we discovered that we had reservations to live in the same complex, so I had an awesome time as soon as I arrived. As it turned out, three other girls from my L.A. life joined them later that month. Theresa Allison, Cara Badger, and Kim Bone also moved into our complex and I immediately felt at home.

School began and it didn't seem too difficult. The campus

was hilly and it was a little tough to get around, but I figured it out quickly and was able to get from class to class on time; when I felt like it. Right before leaving Fresno, I had received my long-awaited van, equipped with a lift and hand controls. I learned how to drive it on the streets of San Luis Obispo, and as my confidence in driving grew, my freedom increased. Unfortunately, I used my freedom to head for the beaches whenever the weather was nice, regardless of my class schedule. I had received one C grade in my life in high school, but when the first one hit in college, they became easier to take.

Unlike most college students, Randy, Sal, and I were pretty well supported financially. We had enough cash to go out to dinner, keep our refrigerators stocked with beer, and basically run amuck, which we did. They had totally taken over my care, including a daily bowel program that involved them having to wear rubber gloves, insert suppositories, and put their hands in nasty places. They never hesitated and we were on our own and having a ball. Occasionally, school would try to interfere with our good times, but it wasn't often we allowed ourselves to be distracted from our social lives. Of course, Cal Poly was on the quarter system and when we got our first report cards after nine weeks, we knew we weren't in Clovis anymore. We had two quarters to shape up or we'd be back home.

In a matter of a few weeks, I had become really close with Moody. Her real name was Michelle, but she'd used her nickname for as long as I'd known her. She had long black hair and dark skin inherited from her Spanish ancestry. Even when we were in seventh grade, she was considered the coolest girl in school. She was also considered the best looking and the years had only made her look better. In fact, all I could think about when I looked at her was that she was the prettiest girl I'd ever seen. Moody loved a good time and we were having fun getting to know each other again. Luckily, living across the lawn from each other, I was able to see her every day. Some time in October, our friendship had progressed to the point that we were dating. It had been only a couple of weeks, but we had a connection. One night, we were partying at our dorm complex, and I ended up in a little stairwell cove with Moody, away from our friends. We started kissing and I was hooked. There was no warning or build up, it just happened. I had figured my days to enjoy moments like this were over. I figured girls like Moody would not necessarily be attracted to me, though I had hope that I could build a relationship with a woman over time. Needless to say, I was pretty excited that Moody returned my affection. She told me later that she never even considered the wheelchair a factor, so I considered myself pretty fortunate. I really liked her, though, and spent as much time with her as I could. For whatever reason, she felt the same and we were a couple from that moment on. We spent time going out to hear my brother play or just going to dinner. Our favorite spot, though, was Morro Bay. We would drive the ten miles late at night and make out at the famous Morro Rock. It was awesome and I was hooked. I had actually begun a relationship with a girl named Lori Shirley before I left for school, but I was in love with Moody. By Christmas, I came home to tell Lori that it was over. Lori was very cool and had been a friend of mine all through high school. We started spending time together right before I left for college, and sparks started to fly. We began dating and it was pretty nice. I was not prepared for Moody to happen, but it happened big.

The education I received from the city of SLO did not come from the university, though. I had a life changing experience with the State of California's local government offices. The social services people from Fresno County had coached me to register for Social Security and Medi-Cal once I got settled at school. They even told me that Randy would be eligible for some pay as my medical attendant; a pretty good deal we thought. Besides the extra cash to support our financial aide packages, the health and medical coverage was important. A trip to the emergency room wasn't uncommon as I learned to know the messages my new body would send. Bladder infections were common and brought high fevers. Any pain below my paralysis caused profuse sweating and blinding headaches. Without Medi-Cal, we would have had to pay cash to get treatment, so we were motivated to get signed up for state assistance. I was told that was how disabled people survived and I quickly discovered why. As we registered for what we thought was a simple entitlement, we were blown away. We filled out forms that asked me to define my day down to the minute. We were more surprised to find the gal from the county office make an appointment to spend the day with me to verify our claims. She mentioned that she needed to see if I was "disabled enough" to qualify for aid. I didn't know what that meant. I was sure that being paralyzed from the neck down would fit the criteria, but she needed to prove it. I was amazed but figured it to be beauracracy at its finest. Imagine the pride when she called later in that week and pronounced me sufficiently disabled, even going so far to tell me she was able to do me favor and give me full credit for my physical needs. Her voice on the other end was so artificial that I wanted to vomit. Her phony laugh as she explained to me that I needed regular care convinced me that she didn't even know who I was. I, however, was getting the money. Wow! What a gift.

There was one other catch she mentioned when Randy and I went in to her office to sign the final forms; a meeting that will live in my mind in infamy. We were asked to sign an agreement that said we'd cut off all relationships with our families. We were certain she meant financial support, so we were ready to agree. She clarified, though, that we couldn't go home for Christmas or any other visit. The premise was if we had any contact with our parents, they were considered financially responsible for us, and we were ineligible for assistance. I hadn't heard that people who needed state aid needed to be adult orphans, and I was flabbergasted. I'm not sure why I was surprised, as we'd already learned that if you tried to do anything that might earn you a dollar, your benefits were terminated. It was clear that this was a system designed to prevent a person with a disability from gaining independence. It promoted total reliance on the government for your basic living expenses and had most people in situations like mine over a barrel. They definitely made it easy to stay home and do nothing, and with the high cost of health care and medical supplies, it was damned near impossible to survive without the system.

Our naiveté allowed Randy and me to sign those forms. Certainly, all that family disassociation stuff was a scare tactic; they'd never follow through on their threat to check on us to see if we ever went home. Anyway, it was mid-November and this process had moved into its second month and we wanted it finished. Finally, everything was resolved and we were scheduled to receive our first check in December . . . in time for us to go home for the three week Christmas break. As promised, the check came and we loaded my van and headed home for the holidays. We were really excited to see our friends. Randy had especially missed Wendi, his girlfriend of three years. We were experienced beach guys now and couldn't wait to tell all of our amazing exploits.

Break was awesome and we wasted little time getting the old crowd together. Most everyone was around and we picked up where we left off. It felt really good to be on my home turf and everything fit like a favorite shirt or sweater. We saw the old football team play for the Championship and win; something we couldn't accomplish. I was touched when we got there and the team surrounded me and we exchanged backslaps. The guy that took my jersey number fifty-four had even put my name on a towel that he wore during the game. It was a great evening, and we knew that there really was no place like home.

I avoided Lori as much as I could. I really liked her but had fallen hard for Moody. I figured if I ignored her the problem would go away, but it didn't. We spent some time together and I decided one night it was time to tell her the truth. Like the punch line of an old joke, she fired the first shot. Lori told me that she had dated regularly and even though I had agreed to that before I left, it hit me wrong. I was stunned, and like a jerk, I was devastated. It was pretty bad to be mad at her even though I was in a full-blown relationship with another girl. Anyway, I did what any sap would do; I begged her to stay with me and swore my allegiance to her. I spent the last days of my vacation following her around like a puppy dog. When I went back to school, two things were clear: I really wanted Lori in my life, and I was terribly homesick.

As soon as we got back to school, the luster of the beach was gone for all three of us. We were terrible students and weren't into the social scene anymore. We went out and had fun, but the novelty of being away from home had worn off and we started nitpicking. The food was bad, the traffic too busy, the weather was cold, and everything was stupid. The truth was, we couldn't handle it and wanted to move home. I tried to string Moody along, but she was too smart for that. She badly wanted a committed relationship and was totally willing to be in a long-term love affair, but I was completely rude and distant to her. In a matter of weeks, she was rid of me, and I knew I hurt her badly. I was so into myself, though, I couldn't treat her honestly. So, I got what I deserved.

The ultimate insult when we got back to school came in a message from the Department of Social Services. They had, in fact, visited us and determined that we went home for Christmas. After one check for me and one for Randy, they were terminating our benefits, including Medi-Cal. I was beyond angry and made a profanity-laced scene on the phone to no avail. I spoke to some clerk who almost certainly did nothing wrong. I called her names and raised my voice to say that I thought, "They were all assholes." I hung up and made a vow to myself that I would NEVER rely on assistance for my life.

I had received a settlement from my accident in the amount of almost two hundred thousand dollars, after lawyer fees, and I pledged to Randy that he'd get paid from that. He shared his money with Sal, so we were fine. In fact, that kind of money to a college freshman allowed the good times to multiply and we lived well. I'd heard somewhere about The Great American Dream and thought for a brief moment that it would be handed to me as payment for my troubles. Clearly, if there was a dream to be fulfilled, it was up to me to make it happen. On that day in my dorm room, I promised myself I'd never be a part of the system. I was going to make mine! That day was one of the single most important experiences of my life and I thank God that the County of San Luis Obispo treated me like dirt.

Our trips home became more frequent, and by the spring we had decided to move home at the end of the year. I took my settlement money and put it as a down payment on a little house in Clovis that would close escrow right about the time we came back. Randy, Sal, and I agreed we'd all move in together and would continue our fun. We really enjoyed each other and as we distanced our-selves from everything and everybody in SLO, we pretty much just had each other. For us, though, that was fine because we were going home. At some level, I found strength in the experience because I learned I could make it out in the world. I could live, make new friends, and even find love away from my comfort zone, and it was reassuring. Since I proved it to myself, I didn't need to impress anyone else. I just had one piece of unfinished business.

The end of the year at Cal Poly was marked by a tradition-al party and concert at our complex. We had drifted away from everyone except the guys in our suite, but we were not on unfriendly terms with anybody. So, we looked forward to a chance to get a little crazy and say goodbye. My relationship with the La Canada girls was good, and Moody and I were at least starting to speak after a chilly few months. Everybody was out and the beer was cold so we had a great time. As usual, Sal was sick after about two beers, but Randy and I were in for the long haul. Late in the day, I finally got the chance to talk to Moody alone. Lori had dumped me in about March and in my effort to have two relationships, I'd been left with none. I, though, at least wanted to try and apologize to Moody for the way I'd treated her. She was amazing, and I didn't deserve her. I had lied, cheated, and blew her off when she really wanted to love me. The only consolation for her would be that I really regretted it and missed her terribly. I told her I was sorry and that, even though it probably didn't matter, I knew I destroyed a wonderful relationship. I think she needed me to say that. She even told me that it DID matter and she forgave me. We hugged and even kissed, and now I was really feeling like I'd made a mistake because I still had a thing for her. I kept in contact with her for about a year, and I even visited her the next year in SLO for a weekend. We went to dinner and visited our old spot at Morro Rock. I held and kissed her and she felt so good. I had no idea that would be the last time I'd see her. I spoke to her on the phone a couple times after that before losing contact. All the other girls graduated from Cal Poly, but Moody ended up transferring to San Diego State and going into sales in that area for many years. She eventually found her way into the airline business and maintained both her beauty and free spirit. I have no regrets about our time at the Coast, but it wasn't all we had hoped. One thing I know for sure, though, was that Moody Cabanillas was the best thing that happened to me in my year long beach adventure. I have never forgotten her or the lesson she taught me-that a woman can love you for your heart, mind, and soul.

June, 1980

One of the best feelings I've ever had was pulling into Clovis from San Luis Obispo to my very own house. I had just turned nineteen, but I was a proud homeowner and suspected that my place might be a hang out for many of my friends. When I rolled in off the highway, my brother Scott was there as were my pals Ray and Criss. Once Randy, Wendi, and Sal showed up, the old gang was back together. I looked around and felt that same safe, comfortable feeling we had in high school at the river. I would enroll at Fresno State in the fall and live in the place where I felt I belonged. At least for now, all was right with the world.

From the first day, I sensed I could accomplish everything I wanted in life from Fresno State. Familiar faces were around every corner and the pace of the semester system seemed much easier than Cal Poly. I was very comfortable and was planning on knocking out my general education requirements before I declared my major. The first semester I was on cruise control and was much more interested in renewing old acquaintances than studying. I was fine with B's and C's, and that was all I earned.

I even briefly re-united with Michelle, my high school love. We had a class together and were soon sitting by each other and walking to and from class with each other. I had been lucky, I felt, that I'd found girls to see beyond my wheelchair and had enjoyed a pretty successful social life. I had yet to take the final step in a relationship and was unbelievably frightened of my ability or inability to have any sexual relationship. One night during this time of my life, Michelle was over and after enjoying dinner we were able to answer those questions. We went into my room and it was inevitable. She looked me in the eye and asked the obvious question, "What do I do?"

I had her help me take my shirt off and wheeled myself over to the bed. She helped me get into bed by standing in front of me and grabbing my belt loops of my pants. She slid my rear over on to the bed and the rest of my body fell out of the chair on to the pillows. I had her roll me from side to side while she undressed me. It was the first time a girl saw me naked and I was too nervous to care. We kissed for a long time, and soon she was lying on me with her clothes in a pile on the floor. I could feel her skin as she rubbed up against me, but only from my chest and higher. She did all the work as I lay on my back. We ended up staying awake all night, and it was very satisfying to me emotionally. Yes, it was awkward. No, it wasn't perfect. Yes, I enjoyed it. And, most importantly for me, YES, I could! We stayed close for awhile, but our relationship never took off again. She ended up marrying fairly soon after we stopped hanging out together and moved away. She was a big part of my young life though, and really did more than anyone else in helping me overcome the fear that nobody could ever love me.

As the spring semester moved slowly along, I was totally uninspired. I was striving for C's by this time and finding it difficult to navigate my van in the direction of the university, which was all of about one mile from my house. Our house, by the way, had lived up to my expectations and we enjoyed an open door policy at all hours of the day and night. The only change was Sal. He never moved in when we returned from the coast and was replaced by my friend Scott. Sal was very close to his parents and wanted to be home. We were still pals and he was a regular at the house, but he preferred his mom's home cooking. Scott, Randy, and I found ourselves hosting parties we never even planned, but we didn't care. Beer and poker were the rituals to which we were faithful. It was fun, but hardly a pathway to success. I was bound and determined to make my way in the world, but I was certainly in no hurry.

My aimlessness reached its peak in the spring of 1981 when I finished the semester with all C's and made the decision to drop out of school. I was on "scholarship" courtesy of the Department of Rehabilitation and was seriously wasting their money. I was about to turn twenty and had lost all interest in school. I really had no plan, but I knew I needed a break from college and I took one. A friend and I concocted a plan to enter the music business. My brother hooked us up with his agent and we joined his artist management company that tried to find places for young musicians to play. I had joined the corporate world at the age of twenty and within two or three short months of hanging out in bars and listening to crappy local bands, I realized how much I wanted a college degree. There was no way I would last as a booking agent. The only positive experience from this venture was learning that bouncers were afraid to ask a guy in a wheelchair for his ID. I wasn't old enough to be in the clubs but was never carded one single time! Unfortunately, that small victory did not sustain me, and I got out of that line of work. My break lasted one semester and I came crawling back to college with my tail between my legs.

November, 1980

*T*wo good things happened to me during this period of irresponsibility. The first was a fluke. I was home in the afternoon when the phone rang. It was Wendi's mom who worked for the Clovis school district. Wendi and Randy had been together since we were fourteen, so Wendi was as much a part of our home as anybody else. Her mom, however, was looking for Scott and he took the call. Apparently, a local elementary school named Fort Washington needed a basketball coach and their season was just days from starting. I was the bigger sports nut, but Scotty played basketball in a recreation league and looked more like a coach than I did, if you know what I mean. By the way, the elementary athletic leagues in our school district are actually pretty serious and winning and losing mattered, as crazy as that sounded. Scott asked if he could have an assistant and he and I became coaches to about sixty young boys in grades four through six, who had no idea what was in store for them. Coach Bohan had always told me that to beat the no-hopes, you had to get out in the world and participate. People would stare, laugh, make fun, and eventually get over it. It was my responsibility to seek and take advantage of opportunity and though this wasn't a ticket to the NBA, it seemed like fun.

The first day, we were stunned to see the numbers of kids, but they were more stunned when they saw us. Their surprise was only exceeded by the shock on the face of the principal when we pulled up. Clovis is a very conservative public school system that, to this day, proudly has a strict dress code for its students. Boys can't have hair longer than their ears, and any earrings or piercings would activate Armageddon. Dr. Richard Sparks was the principal, and he was considered straight-laced, even in

this system. Imagine his surprise when his new basketball staff arrived, both with hair flowing to our shoulders
and fat diamond earrings glittering in the sun. To boot,
one of the guys was in a wheelchair! As he tells the story
today, his only thought was, "What have I gotten myself
into?"

I knew I had a chance when I was introduced to these
ten and eleven-year-old kids and I drove my chair closer
to them. "Cool," was uttered about fifty times so I was
quite the attraction. To them, all they cared about was
how fast my chair could go and if it would do any wheel-
ies. We seemed on the same intellectual level and I was
relieved.

We were quickly assured by a member of the staff that
there was no pressure to win. Fort Washington was a
small school and never won, so it was all about fun. We
had a junior varsity team of about forty players who
played simulated games with other schools. There were
no officials and the kids just rotated until everybody
played. It was organized chaos, but great fun to watch.
The varsity team was comprised of about fifteen of your
best players and they played for real. There were officials,
scorekeepers, and league standings; the works. Scott and
I had a plan to teach our young guys to play defense, contrary to the other young teams who liked to run up and
down the court and shoot. We figured if we kept teams
from doing what they knew, they'd get mad and we would
get steals and lay-ups. For the record, we hadn't the foggiest idea what we were talking about, but we shocked
everyone and won our first four games. Our little squad
of "Hoosiers" was the talk of the elementary scene and
we were having a blast. I think the kids liked it too. Our
highlight was being invited to play an exhibition game
against another unbeaten team before a high school playoff game in front of about two thousand fans who were
louder during our game than they were when the high
school teams played.

We lost by two, but it was over the top.

We ended up the season with a record of six wins and two losses, tied for second in an eight-team league. We actually played what amounted to a championship game and lost in the last seconds. The principal, parents, and kids were really pleased with how much fun we had, so Scott and I got a ton of positive feedback. The real win for us, though, was how much we loved those kids. We built relationships with these young boys that brought me to tears more than once. They treated us like rock stars and giving them success made it even more rewarding. It was the first time in the two years since my injury that my wheelchair was an asset, not a concern. The kids thought I was very cool for having this electric cart that tooled around their school. More impressively, they never defined me as a disabled guy or acknowledged that part of my life. I was Coach Eben and I had a trick ride. As those young boys grew up into young men, I had the chance to see some of them. Several mentioned the fact that I was the first disabled person they ever met, and it taught them some lessons about judging others. One defining moment occurred late in that season when my mom came to a game to see what all the fuss was about. She walked onto the campus and asked a young student for directions. He asked for whom she was looking and she said, "Coach Eben." He walked with her a few steps toward the courts and pointed off in the distance in my direction. "Do you see the guy over there in the cowboy hat?" he asked. "That's Coach Eben." Mom told me that story and I knew I could get used to being the guy in the hat instead of the guy in the chair. When the season ended, Scott and I made sure we were on the list for the next year.

The other good thing from my lazy period happened on a night I was at a party at the college. The term hadn't ended yet and I was technically a student, though that would require a stretch in the definition of the word. We had been partying pretty hard, which is the only explanation of how I ended up at any university function. I never went to any college stuff because I was firmly entrenched in my friends from high school. On this night, however, we chugged a few beers and ended up at the Fresno State amphitheater. My physical situation never affected my ability to handle alcohol, and I tested it far more than I should have. So, there I was, an obnoxious guy in a wheelchair trying to be cool for a bunch of girls who weren't looking my way. Strangely enough, a young girl approached me and introduced herself. She was about sixteen and looked even younger, but she reminded me that she had come to my house one night while she was dating my friend Criss. I remembered her and we made polite conversation for awhile. It turned out I knew her older sister in high school, but that was as far as any connection would go. Her name was, ironically, Michelle, which seemed to be a pattern in my life. In this case, though, I thought nothing of it but a small chat at a party. As she talked she revealed to me that she had a serious crush on my friend Sal. I thought that was pretty funny since Sal was kind of our loveable jester and we always loved to mess with him. Apparently, I told this young girl that I'd help her connect with my pal and made arrangements to pick her up from her high school and take her to lunch. Strangely, I had no recollection of that conversation the next day, but my life was about to change again.

February, 1981

Michelle Mastro entered my life and I could never
have imagined what was ahead for us. She was born in
1964 to Joe and Paulette. Both were well into their forties when she was born and were very European. Her
dad was old school Italian whose parents were born in
Italy. Paulette was born and raised in France and still
speaks with a thick French accent. They met when Joe
was a cook in World War II and he brought her to Fresno
when she was only sixteen. They had two older children
when Michelle was born; a brother Paul who was nine
years older than Michelle and a sister Lilette, fours years
her senior. Most of Michelle's childhood memories involve
working with her mom. Heck, I didn't do any work until
adulthood.

The Mastro family was big on work, short on play. As the
youngest, Michelle would go along with mom to her different jobs. Somewhat of a small business owner, Paulette
owned a pet shop, a boutique, a house cleaning service,
and worked in restaurants and churches. Michelle spent
a large part of her childhood working in these environ-
ments. She wasn't allowed a lot of opportunities to play
outside or spend the night with friends. Her early rec-
ollections come from hanging around her mom, and,
though that seemed completely odd to me, Michelle was
happy enough with her childhood. There wasn't a lot
of affection, though, and she missed out on things like
being held, read to, or going on vacations. They weren't
even real holiday people, so Christmas or other traditions
weren't a part of her youth. Truthfully, though, I had
more trouble with those facts then she did. Our family was big on traditions and held onto them through the
peaks and valleys that come with marriage and divorce.
We knew every Christmas carol and nursery rhyme ever

sung, and it is hard to imagine a childhood without those simplest of pleasures.

Joe was a butcher who worked his entire life in the food and grocery business. He was a hard working man who never cheated his employer out of an honest day's work. Joe was also a character. He was loud, sarcastic, and full of laughs when he was at work or at a function. At home, though, he was quiet and tired, so he didn't spend a lot of time playing with his children. Joe provided well and they wanted for little. He and Paulette, though, didn't believe in spending money so the kids had few frills or luxuries.

The Mastro family was dealt a blow in 1975 that was crippling. Michelle's brother drowned at a graduation party after becoming ill in the pool. In all the crowd of young high schoolers, no one noticed him struggling, and Paul was taken at the age of 17. Michelle was only nine at the time, but has vivid memories of the sadness. To this day, the smell of incense transports her immediately to her brother's funeral as does the song "Ave Maria." As anyone can imagine, the loss was devastating to the entire family, especially Paulette who still passionately misses her son.

As Michelle entered junior high school, she was a doer. She would try out for sports and plays and never was deterred by her failure to make the team or group. Michelle became a clarinet player and did pretty well in band. She enjoyed her early teen years because of her relationships. She'd spend hours at night hanging out with the kids from the neighborhood until her mom would find her to come in. She didn't have much freedom, again, totally contrary to my youth. Her parents were trying hard to put aside their grief, so they didn't have the energy to put into Michelle or Lilette. Her folks didn't attend her school activities or involve themselves in her social life. Michelle would spend her summers with her mom at their beach house in Morro Bay, a beautiful place but not much fun for a teenager who is there for months without anyone her age. So, the times she got to hang out in her neighborhood were precious.

In high school, she didn't have time to be too involved in school activities because she had to start working. It started with a paper route when she was twelve and never stopped. Her throwing the paper would have been something to see. Michelle was born pre-mature and was always small and frail. She never got much taller than five feet, so seeing a tiny young girl on a bike loaded with newspapers had to be a sight in the mid 1970's. She did, however, make some money, which was an expectation. If she wanted clothes, school stuff, etc., she bought it on her own, so she was amazingly independent as she got into her teens. Eventually, she got a job working at my friend's tortilla factory as a bookkeeper and had a second job cooking for some Catholic priests, a job she got from her mom. By the time she was sixteen, her social life was limited, so for her to attend the fraternity party at Fresno State University the night we met was pretty unusual.

To my surprise, Michelle called me a couple days after we met to confirm our lunch plans. It was a good five minutes before I had an inkling of who I was talking to on the phone, but she was female and I acted like I did. We arranged a time and place to meet and I showed up, unsure of whom I was going to see. To my relief, this tiny little cutie walked to my van and I started to remember our conversation from the fraternity party. She had less than an hour for lunch, but we got to talking and soon her returning to school was a distant memory. I had splurged and taken her to Bob's Big Boy Restaurant, and we sat there in deep discussion for hours. When we finally looked up from our conversation, it was late afternoon and we knew each other's life story. I really enjoyed it and asked her if she wanted to have dinner on Friday to continue the visit. She agreed and we had an official first date, though it didn't seem to have any of the strangeness that often accompanies new relationships.

I couldn't take my mind off her all week and when I picked her up, I asked her if I could kiss her? She complied and said she had a question for me as well, "How do you go to the bathroom?" she blurted.

I almost fell out of my chair laughing. It wasn't exactly Romeo and Juliet stuff, but the effect was the same. I couldn't get enough of this girl and she was completely uninhibited by my physical situation. Our evening got off to a rocky start as on our way to the restaurant I got a flat tire. I couldn't fix the flat, obviously, but Michelle was totally amused. There was no awkwardness or embarrassment, and I called Randy and he came to help me. We ended up waiting for him in a grocery store parking lot in full-blown lip-lock. Unfortunately, Randy got there quickly, ending our make-out session and got us fixed. We got on our way and had a blast laughing about our car trouble the whole evening. It was such an easy night that felt really comfortable, and I sensed Michelle was just as relaxed. She came over to visit during the weekend, and I was clearly into something that had my attention. In fact, I told my mom after that visit that I thought this young girl with whom I had little in common would be the girl I would marry.

Michelle and I became a couple and the weeks and months passed quickly. I was out of school and had realized my venture into Corporate America was a dismal failure. I had turned twenty and was watching my friends turn into adults. Randy and Wendi were getting married, as was my friend Ray. When Randy moved out of the house, it marked the end of an era. He had been the best friend I'd ever known and his leaving seemed to signal the end of our youth. Sal moved in with Scott and me and the fun continued, but it wasn't the same. I knew I was on the fast track to nowhere and made plans to re-enter Fresno State. I was nine units short of completing my general education courses, and was ready to approach school with a different attitude. I left the music business, started my second season of coaching basketball and when 1982 arrived, I felt something good was coming. Everyone was genuinely happy for me, particularly over the fact that I had found someone with whom to share my life. Strangely enough, it never occurred to me that our ages could be an issue. A twenty-year-old guy working in the school system dating a minor would cause an uproar in many places. For me, it was a blessing that was totally accepted and even celebrated.

We spent every moment together, either in person or on the phone. We could talk about nothing for hours. My roommates were blown away at how much time we could sit and gab. She was still in high school, so we couldn't come and go as we pleased. The phone became our lifeline, and we used it. When we did get together, we'd hang around sporting events. I was announcing events like baseball and wrestling at my old school, so she would come with me and watch. Michelle also was a regular at the house, and soon we were like an old married couple, as comfortable as could be.

Even as young as we were, marriage came up often. We talked of living together, starting a family, and building a life together. It seemed a natural progression to our relationship for us, though not everyone in our lives agreed. Her dad had immediately thrown up a red flag when he realized this was more than a passing friendship. He confronted Michelle in their home one evening and chastised her for dating a person in my physical condition.

"You'll get tired of him and have to hurt him," he warned her. "You shouldn't be leading him on."

I wasn't too worried about it, but those types of comments hurt Michelle. She desperately wanted a big, happy

95

family but it wasn't going to happen. Her sister Lilette was out of school and working so she wasn't around much. She was a pretty free spirit and did not get along with her mom, so she didn't come home often. Though I had known Lilette in school, we were casual acquaintances at best, and she was mystified at her sister's taste in men as well.

"I don't know how you can go out with someone like that." she told Michelle one day.

Michelle responded with some flippant answer, so she handled it well. It was clear to me, though, that I was not particularly welcome in her home, so I stopped going over. If I did visit the house, we stayed outside and I avoided any confrontations with her folks. Eventually, her mom got very tired of our relationship and called me at home.

"Has Michelle been coming to your house?" she asked in her thick French accent.

"Yes," I replied, "is that a problem?" Her friends had been dropping her off on the weekend nights so we could spend time together. After they had they'd come back and pick Michelle up and take her home.

"I don't want her seeing you," Paulette yelled, "and I especially don't want her going over to your house!"

So, we did a lot of sneaking around. They knew we were a couple, but I never saw them and was totally fine with it. We went about going to school, meeting for lunch and then me taking her to her job. When she was done I'd pick her up and take her home. When we got to her house, I'd slow the car down enough for her to get out, but that was about it. On the weekends, her friends would pick her up and bring her over to my house. They'd go out to a party or something and Michelle would stay with me and hang out. She'd cook dinner, make a fire, and we laid low. That was most of our courtship.

Her parents actually did me a favor by trying to keep us apart. Our fantasy talks about getting married got serious because that was the only way we were going to be together. She was only seventeen when we went shopping for wedding rings and it felt right. We decided to tie the knot right after she graduated, but she wanted her parents blessing. I'm not sure how she got them to come, but Michelle and her folks showed up at a local Mexican restaurant one night in March to meet me. I was sure this night would be ugly, but I was determined.

After some strained small talk, I took a deep breath and let it fly. "I would like to marry your daughter?" I asked pretty matter of factly.

Her dad looked at Michelle and said, "You want to get married?"

She nodded and he responded with, "You're so young!"

To my amazement, Paulette came to our defense. "It doesn't matter, Julie, (a nickname for Julius, his real name)" she blurted out, "remember how young we were?"

I never dreamed she'd be my ally, but at that moment, her words made the difference. Michelle's dad raised his wine glass and said, "Salute!"

We were engaged. The only stipulation was that the wedding be held at St. Helen's Catholic Church in Fresno, where Michelle grew up. I was fine with that, but frankly, I was so relieved that I'd have agreed to get married in a parking lot if necessary. A couple of days later, we had dinner with our friends Kim and Steve, who were newlyweds themselves. Michelle's folks were out of town, so we decided to barbecue at her house. I bought some champagne because we were going to tell them about our wedding plans. Michelle didn't know, however, that I'd pur-chased her favorite ring from our shopping trip. I'd taken it to Kim and she brought it with her to the barbecue. When we opened the bubbly, Steve quickly put the ring in Michelle's glass. As we toasted, her eyes got big and the rest was history. We were getting married in October, some seven months later. There was much to do, but we were excited and our days and nights consisted of plan-ning a big, fall wedding.

January, 1982

I continued my coaching, and leading the young hoop team was as much fun as the first year. The only thing different was Scott's work schedule changed and over the course of the season, he faded out of the picture. By now, I was pretty comfortable around the school and was able to finish largely by myself. Jon's band had dissolved and he was back in Fresno. A devout basketball fan and a pretty good player for an old guy, he helped me a little, but I was mostly on my own. We actually won again and the relationships I continued to develop with the kids were becoming very important to me. When year two ended, the principal had noticed that I was having success with these young people. He offered me an opportunity to return the next year in an expanded role. I was to become the football, basketball, and track coach at Fort Washington giving me a place to go every day from September to June. It seemed a perfect job to have while I went through college and I accepted. I did not know it then, but that would be the defining decision for my career and my future.

My return to school was a success. I had matured and was focused on graduating. I actually cared about my grades, and finished the semester and all of my general education classes. I decided that I still liked the world of journalism and went at the end of the year to take the entrance exam for admittance into the news editorial program at Fresno State. The only classes I did well in my first two years were English courses that required me to write. I was more interested in being a reporter than a broadcaster by this time. Both disciplines were in the School of Journalism, so if I got in, I could explore both which was appealing.

Over the years since rehab, I'd gained limited use of my arms and was getting stronger all the time. When I left the hospital, I was sent home with a few pieces of equipment to help me adapt. One thing I used was a Velcro strap that held a fork or spoon to help me eat. As I looked at that strap, I noticed that if I cut a hole in the end, the fork would go all the way through the little holder. I took a pen and poked it through, and it was just the right length with which to write. So, I'd invented a little device that held a pen and was able to write and survive in school. I was a little slower than most and it was very hard to read, but professors were always willing to work with me. The journalism entrance exam caught me off guard, though, and I quickly fell behind. The proctor, who happened to be the department chairman, was a well-respected educator at the university. He was a towering presence who bordered on intimidating, and as he read words and questions to which we had to respond, I couldn't keep up. I was too proud to ask for help and scrambled to the finish. My heart sank as I waited for the results and when I got my score, I was not surprised to learn that I had failed, blowing my opportunity to continue my education in the only field that had interested me. I rolled out of that room pretty disgusted because I knew the material and felt I could pass under different circumstances. I realized I had nothing to lose and wheeled myself around to ask for a second chance.

Jim Tucker turned out to be a gentle cat. As big and imposing as he appeared, he was very kind and listened patiently as I explained how I knew the answers but couldn't keep up with his pace. I hoped to re-test with him one-on-one to show him I was able. He was very polite as he told me that I would find journalism too difficult. Mr. Tucker explained how they had to write stories daily using the school's antiquated typewriters and he didn't see how I could succeed. Coach Bohan would have never tolerated my quitting anything, so I persisted in my argument. The big guy finally relented, saying he didn't want to ever be seen as not giving someone a fair shot. We rescheduled and I nailed the test.

As I sat in a classroom with him, he spoke to me in a very soft voice. "I think you are going to have a tough time in journalism," he said, "but you've earned the right to try."

It wasn't exactly champagne, but Mr. Tucker welcomed me to the department. Deep down, I knew I'd never let him forget that comment. His doubt was my guarantee that I would graduate and I went into the summer with a new zest for life. I was on a roll.

When September arrived, I was having a blast. School had started at the university and Fort Washington. I rounded up a couple of pals and two teachers from the faculty and we had a football staff. Since I couldn't demonstrate, I talked a lot and the kids seemed to understand. The football was pads and tackle, so I had to be accurate or someone could get hurt. I learned to be patient and methodical and really enjoyed watching the lights go on in the minds of my young athletes. Journalism classes were also enjoyable. I found it relevant and rewarding and found my way in the school. We raised a desk so I could fit my chair under a typewriter. I typed with a stick strapped to each hand with the same type of Velcro device I used to eat and write. I was learning to realize how much I owed the inventor of Velcro, the mother of all inventions for a quadriplegic. It looked goofy, but everyone got used to it and I typed about thirty words a minute. My life was falling into place and I was confident that I'd earn my journalism degree in two years.

October, 1982

Saturday, the ninth of October, was a spectacular morning in the San Joaquin Valley. The sun was blazing and the sky was a perfect blue; one of those fall days you only see in California. I had a house full of visitors who had spent the night after drinking beer and hanging out the evening before. I woke up with Randy and my brother Scott yelling at me to drink a Bloody Mary with them. Sure enough, Randy came dancing into my room with a silver stein and a big piece of celery protruding out of the top. It sounded awful, but I played along and pretended to want to drink it. As Randy got me dressed and into my wheelchair, he set the drink down and I never touched it. My stomach was full of butterflies and alcohol was not going to sit well at ten in the morning. I was bound and determined to be in good form for the day. For, in a few short hours, I was getting married.

As I rolled out into my living room, there was a definite "Animal House" feel to the scene. Beer cans were every-where, as were the semi-conscious bodies of my grooms-men. I had asked nine of my pals to stand with me on the biggest day of my life, including Scott, my brother and Best Man. Actually, he was supposed to share the job with Jon. The two had moved to Hawaii to play music together and had been there for a year or so. Scott made the trip home, but Jon had run into tough financial times and couldn't afford the flight back to Fresno. Neverthe-less, on this morning, there was excitement in the air as everyone woke up and got moving.

I think it was Randy's idea to take my wheelchair and get it washed for the ceremony. He thought it was important to be clean at the church and it sounded like a good idea.

He and Scott picked me up and sat me in my manual chair in the front yard, where I sat and unsuccessfully tried to relax. They loaded my electric chair into my van and headed off to a do-it-yourself car wash around the corner. I genuinely thought those two would be able to avoid trouble for an hour, but I was wrong. Apparently, they sat my chair in the middle of the stall where the cars usually sit. With absolutely no forethought, they turned the hoses onto my ride, neither of them stopping to think about the thousands of dollars of electronics they were about to ruin. They sprayed and sprayed until they both saw something that appeared to be a scene from a bad movie. My chair started to move by itself. It jerked forward a couple of times and spun around in a circle before stopping. When the two of them walked over to the chair and tried to make it go, nothing happened. It appeared to be burned out and there was nothing they could do. Randy and Scott were panicked because that chair was my mobility. They knew I had no other way of getting up and down the aisle, and they were trying to figure out how to tell me that they had destroyed my wheelchair on my wedding day. As they sat and tried to figure out what to do, the chair dried off. After several minutes, they pushed the joystick and it responded. They drove it around the car wash for a minute and it worked. The elated pair elected to pretend that nothing happened and brought the chair home. They both crossed their fingers hoping that nothing crazy would happen during the ceremony. Thankfully, they did not tell me of their little adventure until later. I was already nervous and this would have put me over the edge.

My roommate Scott came from a family that collected cars and owned a beautiful white limousine with red interior. We got to use it for the wedding, and when it pulled up around noon, it was time to go to the church. The guys loaded me into the back of the limo and we were off. The wedding was at two o'clock, but we were going to take some pictures prior to the service. We drove across town and got to the church in plenty of time. As the guys pulled me out of the car, I noticed our priest Father Walt was waiting for me along with another priest. I sat in my chair and politely greeted the man who would marry us. In the Catholic Church, engaged couples go through classes and counseling with the priest, and we had formed a really nice bond with ours. During our sessions, I had told him of a priest named Father John whom I had met when I was in intensive care. Father John, I remembered, was a pretty tough dude who really connected with me in the hospital. He spoke frankly and, as I vaguely recalled, was a great listener. I had been in a lot of pain and despair during those days, but Father John just prayed with me and somehow made me feel better. I hadn't seen him in the years since I left the hospital, but I remembered him fondly. As soon as I looked at the second priest standing in the parking lot where we had parked the limo, I recognized Father John. As it turned out, the two had been friends for years and Father Walt had invited Father John to help officiate our ceremony. I gave Father John a big bear hug and we both were a little misty-eyed. We spoke only for a moment and the two priests went inside to prepare. I was really touched by that gesture and as the music played in the church, I was ready.

All of us guys entered from the side, and we formed a long line that kept me in the wings. They were all in classic black tuxedos and looked sharp as they stood in front of the church. The bridesmaids came in and paired off with a groomsman until the line got short enough for me to emerge from the side in full view of the congregation. It was packed and I scanned the crowd to see who was there. "The Wedding March" interrupted my daydreaming and there was Michelle, coming towards me with a big smile. She was beautiful and I finally succumbed to the moment. As soon as we faced the front of the church for our vows, I started to cry. Michelle was a rock and I was a mess; not the way I envisioned the start of our life as husband and wife.

The ceremony went by in a blur. I remember my brother singing and our friend Shelly did a song. I had also asked Coach Bohan to read some scripture. I had to have him there to celebrate this win with us. Other than that, it was an event that seemed surreal. When it was finally time to kiss the bride, I couldn't believe Michelle stuck her tongue in my mouth, right in front of everybody. The crowd clapped, and as we walked out of the church, people had looks on their faces that made me believe that they had witnessed a wedding that was not normal. I had a feeling that the people were rooting really hard for us to be happy. Of course, we were so young that few gave our marriage much hope to succeed, but for a moment, everyone was in our corner.

The party at our reception was awesome. We had invited about five hundred friends and family, and it seemed like everyone showed. I hadn't seen my godparents in years and they made the trip from Southern California. Michelle has a huge extended family and they were all there, checking me out. Everybody was friendly and happy, so as the DJ started playing and the beer and wine flowed, there was nothing but love in the room. We danced and partied all night long, and Michelle and I were the last people out the door. The limo had gone as planned, and we drove home in my van. We were tired and quiet, but I knew we had made the right decision. In spite of our youth and my physical challenges, we would prove the no-hopes wrong.

October, 1983

Michelle worked part time as a bookkeeper and we lived modestly off her small income and the interest I earned from my settlement. I had another three semesters of college and loved my work with the kids, so we were fine. Sal married about three weeks after we did and helped Michelle with my care for awhile. Soon, she had it down pat and we were very self-sufficient. I was pretty close with my friend Scott Ellis, but he moved back with his parents only about a quarter mile away. How quickly and easily all of our lives had changed. Randy and Wendi were even expecting my godson in February, so we were a scary bunch. Michelle and I settled in for our first Christmas together and I was pretty damned content.

Our entire first year of marriage was great. We were getting used to living together and had fun. I was busy at school and coaching, and she was working. She even got involved with my teams, helping keep score for games and getting to know the kids and parents. We were both becoming members of the elementary school faculty and were making friends with a few of the teachers and their spouses. My brother Scott announced that he was getting married in Hawaii and Michelle and I were pretty excited about the idea. It was a chance for us to travel to the islands together, and it was awesome. Plane travel was a challenge, but it was well worth it to me. I learned that the airlines have something called an aisle chair that is skinny enough to roll down the plane rows to your seat. It wasn't easy because it took two guys to lift me from my wheelchair into the aisle chair. Since I was almost six feet and four inches tall, I was tough to move and found the seats and leg room average at best. Once we got to our assigned row, they lifted me again onto my seat. They boarded me early, so all this happened, thank God, in private. The one potential danger we discovered was almost comical. I had to sit on my inflatable pad to protect my butt on the long flight. After about an hour, I was sweating badly and knew something was wrong. We finally felt the pad and noticed it had ballooned as our altitude increased and was hard as cement. We let a bunch of air out, and I was no worse for wear. We had a good laugh over it, but we also learned a valuable lesson. We got to Hawaii safely and had a great time. Our entire family attended, including my dad. He was Hawaiian and had family there so we got to do some much-needed bonding with him and his relatives.

That trip to Hawaii actually opened up a new world for me. We all spent time hanging out together, which didn't happen too often. When the four of us Eben children were young, our parents spent a lot of time teaching us to sing. They were both wonderful singers, and we were all blessed with the ability to carry a tune. My sister and I could both sing pretty well, but we never did anything with it like Jon and Scott. They had a keyboard player and worked as a trio at the Texas Paniola Café on the North Shore of Oahu. We spent a few of our nights there during that trip enjoying their music. Of course, we also did our best to take in the sights of Hawaii and found time to throw a wedding for Scott.

What I remember most, though, was the time we spent with my dad. It was one of the very few times that all of us were together in our lives since my parents divorced. Even at my wedding, Jon wasn't able to fly back because of finances, so this week was an event to remember. As the week drew to a close, we were sitting around recalling the good old days of our youth and the conversation turned to the Hawaiian folk songs my father taught us as children. In a matter of minutes, Dad pulled out a ukulele and Jon grabbed his guitar. Dad started strumming a familiar tune and, sure enough, we all broke out in a rendition of "King Kamehameha," one of the first songs we ever learned. Not only did we remember every word, we transitioned into the Huke-lau song without a problem. We had such a good time that we decided to sing them at the restaurant on our last night in Hawaii. My dad also taught me a little duet and I agreed to sing it with him during our little family set. My dad was going to do a few songs on the ukulele, so we had about forty-five minutes of material that nobody but us would appreciate. It may sound simple, but that evening sing-along was one of the very few warm, family nights we had in our lives that included our father.

We performed the songs and the small crowd actually ate it up. When my dad and I sang the duet, it went over well and I really enjoyed it. I think it was the first time I'd sung in public since I was the Tin Man in "The Wizard of Oz" in a summer school production after my seventh grade school year ended, days before I moved back to Fresno from La Canada. I enjoyed doing the song so much, and I had a sneaking suspicion that it wouldn't be my farewell performance.

Our trip was a success except for my trying to prove that my push wheelchair could jump down a step at Scott's house. On our last afternoon at Scott's condo, he and I were sipping margaritas in his little family room. Right outside was a little patio (lanai is the Hawaiian term) and it dropped about six inches from the doorjamb. I was in my manual wheelchair (the electric was not able to fly) and pushing was hard for me. After a couple of drinks though, I was successfully pushing myself around his tile floor and becoming very pleased with my strength. I rolled myself as far as the doorjamb, but didn't dare try to push over the bump and down onto the patio. One more margarita, however, and I was ready. Sure enough, I built up some speed and thought I was going fast enough to clear the bump. To my surprise, the chair hit the doorjamb and stopped in its tracks. My body, however, continued forward. I fell face first onto the concrete of the patio as my entire body was thrown from the chair. My wife was screaming as my brother and I laughed hysterically. It took Scott, Michelle, and Scott's bride Ann to lift me back into my chair. My entire face was road-burned and a bloody mess. I was quite a sight the next day in the airport as I was totally scabbed over. I was prepared with an "I fell surfing" story if anyone asked, but they didn't. I would imagine that my appearance created a few interesting conversations behind my back.

We returned home safely and I got ready to begin my push to graduation. I had one full year in journalism under my belt and was doing very well. As our first anniversary came and went, I was into my senior year and getting closer to starting a new chapter of our lives. I started looking for potential jobs and was excited when a position at my hometown newspaper became available. It was a small, weekly paper that hired journalism students close to their degrees so I liked my chances. I made the final two and was disappointed to hear that I came in second. I got angry when the editor said he'd tried to overlook my disability but couldn't. I soured briefly on the profession, but I got over it quickly and continued my education. Graduation was getting closer, and our second holiday season together brought as much satisfaction as the first. In fact, I hardly even noticed when I caught a cold right after New Year's Day.

January, 1984

I had been warned that colds were dangerous to my
system, but I wasn't overly concerned when it persisted.
Our semester recess lasted until the end of January,
and I had plenty of time to recover in time for the second
semester. It started to get harder to sleep and the illness
was spreading into my lungs, so I knew pneumonia was
coming. I had been through it once before and it was
painful. My stomach muscles didn't work from the paralysis, so I couldn't cough naturally. That allowed the
virus to sit in my body and spread. I would try lying over
the sink and coughing, but it didn't help. We'd lie in bed
at night and Michelle would spend hours pounding on my
chest and belly to force the mucus out of my body. It was
pretty romantic stuff for newlyweds.

The days rolled on and I wasn't getting better. Even the
doctor was worrying. He started ordering tests and had
me poked and prodded in every place on my body trying
to find a reason that I wouldn't heal. I was medicated ex-
tensively, but nothing offered more than temporary relief.
I'd have a good day and think it was going away, then
relapse. I was into the basketball season with my kids
and was trying to hang in there, but had to miss a lot.
Luckily, my pals that I'd recruited to help me with football stayed on for basketball and covered for me. I was
getting pretty scared. Finally, as school was just starting
up again, my pneumonia calmed down and I was able to
start my classes on time. Other than losing weight and
being a little weak, I was fine and on the mend. I had
dodged a bullet and was ready to move on. That is why
I was confused when I got a call from my physician who
scheduled an appointment to see me for a consultation.

My mom knew my doctor from her nursing experiences, but I was still pretty angry when I went to my appointment and found her in the office waiting for me. I was a grown man and didn't need my mommy, so I was a little put out before he even opened his mouth. It was only seconds, though, before I knew this was not a normal visit. The doctor had received my chest X-rays and saw something alarming. It seemed the exam showed something blocking my rib cage. A closer look made my doctor determine that I had a tumor near my chest and needed to see an oncologist that he had already arranged. I was cool at first because I had no idea what oncology meant and saw no need for alarm. I was curious enough to ask, however, and he had my full attention when I learned I was seeing a doctor whose specialty was treating patients who had been diagnosed with cancer.

Michelle and I left the office in a daze as it appeared our honeymoon was over. Breaking my neck had been a pretty dark day and changed my life forever, but I never spent a lot of time asking "Why me?" I totally accepted that it could be me as easily as it could be anyone, and even was proud of the fact that I was being given a test, which I was clearly passing. In the early days, there were the challenges of accomplishing a daily task that kept me motivated. I wanted to eat without help, lift a little more weight, and learn how to write; all kinds of things that kept my mind busy. I remember one night, as I laid on the couch in the first weeks of being home, when I got frustrated. I had peed on the couch for about the third time that day and had enough. I cried and yelled, "What did I do wrong?" I never got an answer, but that fear never really returned. I stayed busy and lived as normal a life as possible, so I didn't have a bunch of lonely times to ponder the fates.

I must admit, though, hearing the word "cancer" was a new ballgame and I did not want to play. Selfishly, I felt strongly that I had endured enough tragedy and it was someone else's turn to be tested. Sure enough, though, the cancer specialist saw the picture, examined me, and confirmed that he "didn't doubt" that I had the C word. Coach would have really been disappointed in me because for the first time since 1977, I had a hard time finding a win on that day.

Just to add insult to injury, I was in serious financial trouble. I had hired an accountant to help me manage my money from my settlement. I had no idea what to do, and our family tax man seemed totally trustworthy to help me. He advised me to put most of my money, about one hundred fifty thousand dollars, into a ranch project he was managing. He had a group of investors who bought fifty acres of raisins, and I was putting up my money as the second mortgage. In a matter of months, the project went bad and the owners defaulted on the payments, losing the property. The ranch was given back to the original owner, but since the second mortgage was secured by the group they were responsible for paying me back. Unfortunately, they were broke and I was out of luck. They couldn't pay me back and I lost everything.

I had no money and, since my unpleasant dealings with social services in San Luis Obispo, I had no insurance. I had been cut off from Medi-Cal and hadn't the foggiest idea of how we were going to pay for cancer care. Luckily, my family doctor was very gracious and worked with me through the pneumonia. He charged me nominal fees and I was able to pay cash for all his services. I was entering a different world in relation to this cost, and Michelle and I entertained the notion that we could lose everything we had. Of course, people die from cancer, so the cost wasn't the most important thing, but our lives were pretty dark. Michelle took two jobs to try to get by, but we were in a situation that was far bigger than we could handle and we needed help. In a miraculous turn of events, it turned out the lead physician of this group who owned the facility was a parent of a young student at Fort Washington. He got involved and we charted our course of treatment, none for which we would be charged. I guess that Coach was right again; no matter how bad it seemed, there was always a win and we definitely found a big victory that helped ease a pretty scary burden.

The first order of business was to find the tumor and identify its type. Once that was completed we'd do the chemotherapy or radiation stuff, but nothing would happen before a biopsy was performed. I had a few weeks before the procedure and spent the time coming to grips with this deal. I decided to fight like hell, so I went to school and took a leave for the rest of the semester. I was close to completing my degree and this would push back my graduation, but that seemed very irrelevant. I stayed sane by coaching the kids, and when word spread of my new battleground, I had hundreds of pint-sized soldiers that had my back. Coaching more than basketball had introduced me to most of the upper grade population at the school, and we were just beginning track season as this heated up. I was coaching young boys and girls and getting a daily education on unconditional love. The strength I got from them was priceless.

The biopsy came and, other than being a little scary, wasn't awful. I was awake the whole time and listening carefully as they took the needle and drilled into my rib cage. I could hear the bones scrape, but it didn't hurt. The big fear, they warned me, was poking a vital organ and collapsing my lung. The way my medical luck was going, I would have put money on the lung collapse, but it didn't happen. I went home in good shape and waited a couple more weeks for the results.

I was pretty discouraged when I got the call in April that my biopsy results were inconclusive. Counting the pneumonia, I'd been living at the doctor's office or hospital almost every day for four months. I was always carrying around a pretty heavy dose of fear about my mortality, so

114

I wanted something tangible. Unfortunately, there was nothing to talk about and we shifted to the next step; I was scheduled for surgery.

I was the best man in my friend Scott's wedding in early May and the surgery was scheduled the next week. I was blown away when I was wheeled into the operating room and again told that I would be awake through this process. What surprised me was the magnitude of what the doctor described didn't seem like a local anesthesia type of thing. I learned that they were going to open my shoulder all the way so they could expose my ribs. The same fear of the collapsed lung was the reason I had to be awake.

I lay on that table for what seemed like hours. I was turned on my side and listened as the sound of cutting and grinding echoed in my ear. At one point, they actually folded my shoulder above my head, an image that was far worse than the reality. They took what they wanted and folded me back together. My back was stitched and in a short time, I was sent home. I was a pretty sore boy and being lifted into bed that night was a challenge. Other than that, the surgery went well and I waited a couple more weeks for the results.

To the dismay of my wife and mother, I got up the next day and took off in my van. I was in some pain, but it was manageable. I took my tuxedo back from the wedding and headed out to Fort Washington for track practice. The season was coming to a close and I didn't want to miss any more, so I was glad to be there. The more time I spent with these kids the more I enjoyed myself. I found that I would make up reasons to go over there early or stay late. That little school had become my refuge and I couldn't get enough of it.

I remember a young blonde boy named Mike. He was a handful, but a smart kid and a good little athlete. He and

I were close and I got a note from him at school one day. It read, "I heard you were sick and I felt bad. I heard later you had cancer and I felt bad again. I hope you get better and come back. Love, Mike." Not exactly Hemmingway, but beautiful in its simplicity. To me, that note meant more than any gift I could have ever received. I loved those kids.

I knew something was up because the principal came out to practice and wanted to show me some documents. The more he talked the more I realized that nothing he said had anything to do with me. I saw the photographer in the distance and knew I was being set-up, but I didn't know why. I was invited to the end of the school year rally under the premise of having to present some athletic awards. When I got there, kids had painted signs with my name and were yelling cheers for me. It turned out they had dedicated their yearbook to me and the whole school showed up to present it to me. I was blown away by the gesture and knew that my life was taking an unexpected detour. I was starting to realize that I was in love with elementary school life.

I'm not sure of the exact date, but it was early June when my phone rang. I was in my bedroom getting ready to do my bowel program in the early evening and it was my oncologist; I was well aware of that term by now. It seemed unusual to be receiving a call at night, but very little was normal in my world anymore. After exchanging the usual pleasantries, he said he had the results from my surgery. What had appeared to be a tumor blocking my ribs was not a tumor at all. It turned out that part of my rib had eroded, which the doctor explained was very normal in some people over time. The rib wasn't blocked, it wasn't there. After six months of indescribable doubt and fear, I heard the words that sounded very musical, "You don't have cancer."

I called my mom and the word spread in minutes to my

family and very close friends. We all breathed a sigh of relief, but mine was surely the loudest. I can't really say that I ever felt like I was going to die. It never got that far and I never felt sick. What was stressful was the uncertainty and the feeling that my life was suspended in mid-air. I went to bed that night and slept soundly for the first time in months. I was finally able to look forward to tomorrow with that same hope that saw me through rehab and helped me scratch my itch. Before I nodded off, I did remember to add a big capital W to my life's win column.

June, 1984

I woke up to a bright day, both literally and figuratively. The phone was a regular companion as people called to verify the good news. One of the callers was my father who shared his happiness with me. He had a little different message than the others, though. He and his wife Pam had booked a three-week trip to Hawaii that was scheduled to begin on June twenty-third, a day before my birthday. For some reason, they were unable to go and could cancel their hotels but not the airline tickets. Dad said after my experience that I could use an island getaway. I thought about it for about one second and jumped all over this opportunity. Jon had moved back to the mainland by now, but Scott and his wife Ann were still there. His new house butted up to the sand on a beautiful stretch of the famous North Shore beaches. I hadn't seen him throughout this whole ordeal but we kept in constant contact on the phone. We had shared a bedroom throughout our lives and were best friends and life-long opponents in driveway sports like whiffle ball, Nerf baseball and football, and one-on-one basketball. For good measure, we mixed in daily boxing matches that featured everything except gloves. Our mother called it fighting, but those bouts made our bond as thick as anything else in our lives. A few weeks with him served me very well.

We arrived in Hawaii and were greeted on our first morning with a birthday party Scott threw for me. He invited all of his friends, none of whom I'd ever met. They brought gifts, a cake, and the whole nine yards, and it was extremely cool. Scott's wife was very pregnant with their first, a boy they were naming Jeffrey. I was really flattered, but Michelle was a little bummed. We wanted a family and thought we'd name our son after his dad; if we

119

were lucky enough to be so blessed. Her disappointment didn't last long and she spent most of the trip sharing in Ann's excitement over the baby.

Our three weeks were pretty good therapy. We spent some time down in Waikiki, mostly at night while Scott played music in one of the beach hotels. Michelle spent time with Ann talking about motherhood and relaxing in the sand. Scott and I even got into a screaming fight one night, just like the good old days. The lion's share of our days, though, was spent in their incredible backyard. Right out the back door was sand for about twenty yards. The waves rolled right up to within ten feet of their house, and if you parked your lounge chair just right, you could sit in the sun while the Pacific Ocean rinsed you off every few seconds. I lay on that beach hour after hour, day after day. Scott would pick me up and lay me right on the sand. He'd build a little mound under my head for a pillow and I was pretty comfortable. I could see only water for miles, just like an island postcard. At the end of the day, he'd pick me up and sit me in a lounge chair, buck naked under an outdoor showerhead on his patio. I had sand in parts of my body that were very hard to clean, but I didn't care. Laying on the beach for several days was exactly what I needed. I spent a lot of time alone in my thoughts, very appreciative of this trip. It was much better than the long, strange trip I had just completed.

August, 1984

I started to feel like a real journalist as I returned for my senior year after my semester leave from hell. My colleagues and I were getting close to graduation and talk was turning to resumes, interviews, and employment opportunities. Fresno State had an excellent reputation across the country for its journalism program, so there was plenty of work in the world of news reporting. I, however, was constantly hearing that most starting jobs were at small newspapers where reporters had to wear many hats including photographer, layout editor, and other roles that required mobility and dexterity. The message was becoming clear that there was doubt from my teachers about my employability.

The journalism department was not a huge place, and certainly, those of us who were seniors had at least a casual relationship with one another. I was actually one of the lesser-involved students in the program. I had declared my major later in my college career and had missed a semester, so I wasn't around very consistently. When I was around, my life was very different from my peers. I was twenty-three-years old, at least a couple of years older than the other seniors. Being married, I wasn't in the social circle of the other students by choice. Michelle and I had both grown up in the immediate Fresno area, so all of our friends and relatives were outside of the college world. Still, I had been warmly greeted upon my return and certainly felt that the teachers and students at school were rooting for me, if nothing else.

I still had one more year, I figured, to coach at Fort Washington. I was one of the veteran staff members of this growing, changing school and really felt like part of the family. The Fort was one of the oldest schools in the district and had for years been way out in the country. It was close to a country club of the same name, and served a small, economically successful clientele. As building in the area grew out to the school, high income houses had surrounded the campus, bringing many two-parent, professional families who supported education, but loved and demanded being successful. In a school district that believed in competition, our little athletic program had grown into a powerhouse and I was getting far too much of the credit. What WAS true was the fact that I was building very meaningful relationships with the students, parents, and staff that would be hard to leave after I graduated and joined the work force.

My maternal grandparents were both teachers, as was my father. My mother's career as a registered nurse had evolved to teaching, so I was surrounded by plenty of influences in the teaching profession. It was such a natural fit; I'm not sure why I'd never seriously considered myself a career educator. I certainly had no intention of starting to change my course now. I'd come this far and I was ready to graduate, so there was nothing to discuss. I was flattered to hear from parents, though, who told me that they wished their children could have me in the classroom. Sadly, it wasn't going to happen because I was a journalist. There was no doubt about it.

Dr. Sparks, the principal who couldn't believe he brought a long-haired, earring-wearing kid to his school had become my biggest advocate and friend. He wasn't a sports fan, but he enjoyed the success of my teams. Even on a stage as small as elementary school sports, winning was fun and added to an already positive school climate. He started to tell me that teaching was a profession I should consider and even went as far as to say he'd love to hire me to teach at Fort Washington. A friend of mine on the teaching staff even let me know that I was lunch room gossip from time to time. There was debate on whether I could handle teaching if and when I got my credential.

122

He shared a conversation where one of the veteran teachers asked him if I was going into teaching. My friend had told her that I was a journalist and she seemed relieved. He told me that she doubted if I could be effective in the classroom because I couldn't hold a piece of chalk. I wasn't sure, but I had hoped there was more to teaching than chalk possession and technique, but she was the veteran. I did, however, sense a challenge and my friend assured me I could succeed. That was also nice to hear, but it wasn't going to happen because I was a journalist. There was no doubt about it.

My senior classes at school afforded me the opportunity to start having stories published in our student newspaper at the university. I wrote a lot of sports pieces initially and really enjoyed the work. The pieces were positive, and athletes and coaches enjoyed the attention. A friend of mine who I'd known from high school was as big a sports junkie as I was, and we partnered on a couple of features on the Fresno State Bulldog men's basketball team, at that time a regular in the Associated Press' Top Twenty teams in the nation. We had total access to the sold-out games and regular contact with Bulldog coach Boyd Grant, a class act, who was easily the most popular citizen in Fresno. Coach Grant had taken time out of his season the prior year to call and wish me well when I was going through the cancer scare. All of this seemed big time and I was feeling like I was a journalist. There was no doubt about it.

We were in a big election year, and my last test for being a reporter was to participate in the coverage of the Reagan-Mondale presidential contest. My job was to cover the campus democrats and I'd done an initial feature story on the president of the student-led group as the debates and campaigns were in full swing. The final piece involved hanging out at the democratic headquarters during election evening and documenting reactions as the results of the voting were reported. I also would interview the democratic student chair again and get his thoughts as the night progressed and his long journey to get his candidate elected ended. Strangely enough, I was a strong Republican, one of the few in the disabled population. I was way out there too, because I didn't like the Democrats policy on public assistance. I thought they gave too much money away to people like me and discouraged education, work, and personal accountability. To me, it seemed wrong to pay more benefits to the disabled the less we did. Social Security and Medi-Cal were taken away if you tried to work at all. So, you were rewarded for doing nothing. Obviously, the more dependent on the system, the more likely you would vote Democrat. I struggled with that philosophy and chose to fight for the other side. It was good practice to cover the Democrats, though, because I had to put my opinions aside and report what I saw. I actually enjoyed it. For realism, we had a midnight deadline so we had to come back to school and work late at night. This was real world journalism and I was right in the middle of the excitement. There was no doubt about it.

We reported to school before we went out to our assigned spots at about five in the afternoon. Our professors gave us a little pep talk, which reminded us that, no matter what, get the story. The televisions were on in the classrooms and when the first network projected the Reagan landslide win at about quarter after five, the excitement of the evening dimmed. Sure enough, the "celebration" planned at the democratic headquarters was sparsely attended at best and the election night buzz never materialized. I sat by myself for hours and had nothing, which became the story. I was able to interview my guy, but it was nothing earth shattering. I went to school and struggled to craft something with some redeeming value. I met the deadline and got my story run, but I was less than enthused. Apparently, life as a journalist wasn't always exciting. I was starting to have doubts about it.

March, 1985

At the time I started my final semester of school, I wasn't that pumped about graduation. It shouldn't have been that easy for one negative experience to spoil my enthusiasm, but I sure wasn't as motivated. My last writing class was a public affairs course and I spent my final couple of months in college chasing boring stories involving disputes that were playing out in city council or boards of supervisor meetings in our area. We had one good project left that was certain to end my educational experience on an exhilarating note. Our very popular mayor had not run for re-election and a cast of political nobodies ran for the city's top office. November had not produced a winner and there had to be a run-off in March to decide who would be Fresno's mayor.

I was pretty pleased to be given the assignment of covering the front-runner. He had known my parents many years prior so I recognized his name. My hand shot up first when the assignments were doled out, so I got the good story. Like in November, I was to hang around his party and find a story based on the results of the evening. I showed up at the local restaurant hosting his gathering and was encouraged at the energy. The crowd was large and a buzz was generated when the results started coming over the television. This candidate was building a good lead and by the end of the night became the Mayor of Fresno. To my surprise, he only granted one of the many interview requests fielded by his campaign staff, and I was the lone reporter given the chance to sit with our new Chief. He remembered me as well and helped me out. I was very grateful and spent a very quiet hour talking about his campaign and his hopes and dreams for the city.

I was pretty proud when I went back to school and wrote my story. I thought I captured well the positive tone of the evening, and my story reflected an optimism that seemed to come whenever a new administration took office. I was stunned when I came to class a couple days later and found my scoop totally rejected by my professor. He spoke to me with clear disappointment in his voice that bordered on disgust. He thought I was soft and gave our new mayor a free pass. He continued to show me quotes from my story and wondered loudly how I could let him get away some of these statements. He told me that if I wanted to be successful in this business I had to be willing to go after people and challenge them at all costs. My lack of motivation was starting to make sense to me. I wasn't sure that journalism was all it was cracked up to be and my doubts were growing stronger each day.

When May came, I donned my cap and gown and headed to Bulldog stadium for my college graduation. I picked up my friend Jeff, who had been experiencing his own life odyssey and took the same long path to this moment as I had. We chuckled at being old men at twenty-four, but we were both pretty proud. We parked and agreed to meet after the ceremony and I found my place among the other journalism grads. The excitement was in the eyes and voices of all of my colleagues as our futures stared us right in the face. My family was among the thousands in the stands who stood and cheered as we marched onto the field to receive our degrees. I was painfully under-whelmed, but I chalked it up to anxiety and put a brave front on for the festivities.

Near the end of the hoopla, the university president made his way through the list of schools and conferred upon each of their graduates the appropriate reward. When he got to the School of Arts and Humanities, we turned our tassels and I had earned my Bachelor of Arts degree in Journalism. I had stuck it out over the long haul and accomplished a major goal in my life. Certainly, Coach

Bohan would be ecstatic as this was a huge win. Why wasn't I?

As the ceremony wound down, I actually wheeled away from my department's seating area. The backslapping was beginning and I felt completely out of place. I didn't really know these people that well and had no job lined up. I wheeled across the field even as the speeches were not finished. I wanted to find Jeff and celebrate this milestone with him. By the time I reached his area, the ceremony was over and the crowd was coming onto the field. I knew I wouldn't be able locate him in the mob, so I headed back. Michelle was the first to find me and her pride was overflowing. She had a little thermos she'd filled with champagne and we toasted the end of this chapter of our lives. I would start earning a living and she could quit her job and start her college career. Michelle was a bookkeeper and dreamed of becoming an accountant. She'd put her dream on hold for me and it was now her turn. All I needed to finish the deal was a job.

Leaving Fort Washington was looming, but since my graduation was in May, I had a few weeks until my job there was finished. I was asked daily what my post-college plans were and I kept saying I was looking for work. That comment was almost always followed by a remark about becoming a teacher. I had worked too hard, though, and wanted to give my new degree a chance. Besides, it took six years to finish school counting the two semesters I'd missed. There was absolutely no way I was going back to school. When Dr. Sparks told me of a special program that allowed college graduates to earn their teaching credentials in one year, I never wavered. I did agree to look into the program and called one of our district superintendents to schedule a meeting. All I wanted was some information, though. I was not going into teaching.

A reporter job opened at the Merced Sun Star, about an hour north of Fresno. I applied and was pleased when they called me for an interview. I took my portfolio of articles and drove the hour until I found the newsroom. I had to take a test and wait for my results. The exam checked my spelling, editing, and writing skills and I breezed through it easily. I knew I'd done fine, but I was still relieved when I got to meet with the editor and he said I aced the test. We had a really productive conversation that lasted for almost an hour. When I left and drove home, I was confident that I would get the job. He told me he'd call me in one week and I waited.

I kept my meeting with the school district official to be polite. I'd known this man for years, even going to kindergarten with his son, so I didn't want to be rude and a no-show. Wendi's mom, who got me that first basketball job years ago, was his secretary so I was in friendly territory when I showed up for my meeting. I'd been surprised before, but few moments in my life left me as speechless as this encounter.

Dr. Kent Bishop did not mince words. He challenged my thinking, my motivation, and my manhood. He reminded me of my heritage and told me that teaching was in my blood. Dr. Bishop yelled, cursed, and pushed me to look into my heart and ask what that particular organ wanted to do. I sat across his desk and felt like a sixth grader when he started raising his voice. "What are you thinking?" he asked loudly. "Your father is a teacher, your mother is a teacher, your grandparents were teachers, and you are a God-damned teacher!"

He was so convincing, I believed him and didn't dare tell him that my mom was a nurse. I was genuinely surprised when he called Fresno State's School of Education to see if they would accept me into Option Four, the one-year program Dr. Sparks had told me about. They had room and would welcome me with open arms, not really a surprise since the Clovis school district was one of their main partners and the relationship was pretty important to the university. The program was housed on one of the district's elementary campuses and several other schools were used for the placement of student teachers. I told him I'd think about it and got out of there while I still had my self-esteem in tact. At least I had a fall-back position if I couldn't get a job, but I was not prepared for that discussion, nor did I expect the debate in my head that took place over the next few days.

It had started so innocently. I was a kid myself looking to kill a few hours a day coaching a twelve-year-old children's basketball team. Even when the job expanded to include football and track it was just plain fun. It wasn't serious and it was never meant to be a career path. Why, then, was my heart telling me that Kent Bishop was right and education was in my blood? All those years in college training to be a news reporter and the thought of not being able to play every day with elementary aged children was really depressing? Finally, after all the ups and downs in my life spent trying to accomplish the goal of finishing school, how could I be seriously considering going back to Fresno State for one more year? Michelle would kill me if I put off earning an income for another year, wouldn't she? Clearly, I knew the right thing to do and I eagerly awaited the call from Merced that would cement my future.

I got the call from the Sun Star editor exactly when he promised. He had given the job we talked about to another applicant. He went on to tell me that he had something even more to my liking. They had a daily and a weekly paper, and he wanted me to be the Sports Editor for their weekly edition. This was exactly the job I hoped for, doing sports, the thing I loved the most. I profusely thanked him for the opportunity but informed him I couldn't take the offer. I never looked back or regretted not taking that opportunity. Indeed, I was a blankety-blank educator. I hung up and called Kent Bishop and within minutes, I was enrolled in Fresno State's credentialing program. I decided to listen to my heart which told me that I wanted to be a teacher. Frankly, there wasn't even any doubt about it.

the EBEN Family Album

How Many Wins
Have YOU Had Today?

The Photo History

B.C. (Before Crash)

My father and I in the Sierras
a few months before my injury.

The Eben brothers trying
to look tough.

My first date ever,
Tish went to a dance
with me despite
my broken
leg.

Carol was
my Sadie
Hawkins date,
...way too classy
for me.

Brother Scott and I on the high Sierra's trip

1

A.D. (After Disaster)

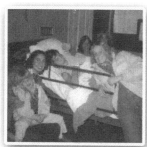

Kim and my friend Gail were two of my constant pals during my rehab.

Dale and his mom visited our home right before his passing.

We were looking good for our Junior Prom.

I led our class into our Senior Farewell Rally.

Randy and I were stylin'.

Catherine Gunst and I went to several functions together. She was a huge part of my life.

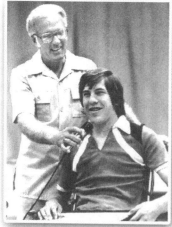

Mr. William Contente was the coolest principal...ever.

Hangin' out at home, fresh out of the hospital...pretty scary.

The Winners In My Life

I dated Lori after graduation from high school and she's still a big part of my life.

Michelle Petereit was a true love and made my recovery easier.

The gang grew up and got married ...and stayed pals.

Wedding day with my partners.

We all aged pretty gracefully, didn't we? Most of us?

My secretary Cathy became my most trusted colleague and great friend.

Moody and Shelby in Aspen. She was one in a million.

3

Coach Eben

My first football team. This group is over 30 now.

I had fun coaching track and some of these kids had great college and pro careers

Celebrating a championship at Clovis West was great fun!

My basketball team **was undefeated and went on to great high school glory.**

This was one of my favorite groups. They seriously over-achieved.

Feel the Love, I Get Paid For This

Miss Brittany Smith came up with our moto and taught me a good lesson.

Kermit was a hit with my elementary students.

I was decked out with Alyssa Takeda for this shot ... a proud moment.

Brother Jon and I entertaining my elementary school carnival.

This cat in this hat is very over-paid.

A recent picture at Courtney's wedding; these beauties were students of mine when they were in sixth, seventh, and eighth grade.

Our staff in my first teaching year became my good friends.

5

The Love Shack Is Born

An artists rendering of Clovis East that turned out pretty accurate.

Our first graduation was an amazing night.

A post 9/11 moment of silence remains my proudest work accomplishment.

My first full management team at Clovis East. We grew up together.

6

The Eben Family Album

The Eben siblings together in Hawaii.

We did a set of music with our dad on the islands.

Michelle and I with my folks on the big day.

When we first started dating, we snapped this shot with Michelle's mom.

Our wedding party resembled a large choir. It was cool, though.

Our Family Grows

Dad, Jared, and Noelle. They were my favorite passengers.

Noelle in her favorite seat.

I dont think Jared walked until he was about eight.

Our first family photo and looking very young.

All Grown Up

Master musician, Jared's Senior Night with the band.

We all are showing some age in this family picture, especially the guy in front.

Noelle got old enough to break her dad's heart.

The last ever complete family picture, including our dad, at niece Breanne's wedding to Jon Ice.

August, 1985

*T*here were about twenty-five of us who reported to a classroom reserved for our program on the campus of Pinedale Elementary School. We came from all different walks of life and took very different paths to this place in our lives. The common ground was life experience. Everyone in the program had done something else or planned a different course in life prior to exploring teaching. At twenty-four years old, I was one of the youngest class members and was one of only two or three who hadn't actually begun another career. It was an eclectic group who had a lot to offer each other.

The program was very simple. We had all passed the necessary tests to teach in California and had completed the required paperwork. All that stood between our classrooms and us was nine months of a small amount of coursework and three different student teaching experiences. At the end of this year, we would hopefully learn more about the craft of teaching and define the types of educators we hoped to be.

Early on we were asked about our own educational philosophies and I wrote some meaningless jargon that I'd heard somewhere, but really was unprepared to explore that part of my brain yet. I was more intrigued by the discussions that revolved around our reasons for pursuing teaching. For me it was simple; I'd had a ball working with young kids and fell in love with the concept of school. I'd been given so much in my own education from adults and children and my coaching experiences that continued to enrich me. Young kids made me happy and that seemed reason enough to be a teacher.

We were also asked what we hoped to give to teaching and

I didn't know the answer to that one. Up until this point, my rationale had centered on the joy I got from school. I knew that I had a good life story and most people would benefit from seeing someone in a wheelchair working along side the able-bodied in a critical profession, but that was as much as I thought to offer. I had a lot to learn about myself, and I was ready.

I was so comfortable at Fort Washington the thought of my first placement being someplace else was very unnerving. I knew I would look very different than every other teacher the children had ever seen, and I was afraid of the commotion I would cause when I wheeled into class on the first day. Thankfully, I drew strength from my San Luis Obispo days and knew my butterflies would eventually pass and I'd fit in. I was assigned third grade and thought that was young, but the point of the three student teaching assignments was to see different people and places, so I reported for my first nine-week stop.

John Burroughs Elementary School served over one thousand students in the southeastern part of Fresno. Every student was on the free and reduced lunch program and impacted by poverty. They were a beautiful rainbow of white, black, Hispanic and Asian students; diversity I'd not seen. It didn't take long to see how different it was than Fort Washington and I was fascinated by the environment created by the teacher.

Doris Force had taught for many years and was nearing retirement. She was a local legend and had tricks and practices up her sleeve that made teaching look easy. Everything had a purpose and she left no stone unturned in her daily routines. I absorbed as much as I could and ate lunch with Doris every day to talk about teaching. It was in those conversations that I discovered her instructional ability was only part of her story.

I spent my time learning the stories of these children and

watching in amazement as they showed up smiling and eager every day. Over the next few weeks I learned that the only time they ate was when the school fed them. Some students weren't taught hygiene and had lost teeth to rot or came without bathing for days. It was normal to see these youngsters in the same unkempt clothes every day or show up in the cold without a coat or sweater. Worse yet, Mrs. Force explained that if I came back in June, half of the class will have moved because their parents can't pay rent and they are forced from their homes. I'd leave every day with my heart in my throat wondering if anybody loved these kids or if there was any point in their dreaming about a bright future?

When I finished that nine weeks, I knew some of the answers to my questions. I watched Doris Force hug each of her students every day for something. As she walked around the room, she would lovingly place her hand on the top of their head, eliciting a smile by a child who knew she cared. When she needed to, she'd be firm and hold them accountable but never moved on without teaching a value or re-affirming her belief in the young boy or girl with whom she was dealing. Mrs. Force spent plenty of her own money as she always had little treats that were more valuable than gold to this particular group of seven and eight year olds. I was even impressed with the principal who was everywhere. He talked daily about how good these kids were and they believed him.

So, I left that school with a wealth of activities and strategies that would help me teach better. I had a significantly better understanding of the point of teaching that I really appreciated. I learned that we don't teach for ourselves. We have young people who need us and sometimes, we are the only people they have. Doris Force loved those students and she gave them hope every day. She was not able to fix their homes, heal the pain of divorce, or get parents released from prison. She was able to make sure that every minute those kids were with her they was filled with some magic. They loved her and I was proud to think I could be going into something that was far bigger than I realized.

I learned one painful thing on the last day I was there. As I was saying goodbye, the principal who had given so much positive energy to his community was led away in handcuffs in front of everyone. His face was on every newscast and in every local paper for days. It turned out he had hidden cameras and was taking pictures of little girls changing. He was accused of other molestation charges and eventually sent to prison. I'll never forget the hurt and betrayal on the faces of the students and staff. It really pounded into me the responsibility we must demonstrate because of our positions of trust. As awesome as it is to have the ability to touch people's hearts, it is even more devastating when we break them.

My second stint was about as different as could possibly be. I moved just prior to the Christmas break to Kastner Intermediate School in Clovis. This school was a high-performing, high-income school serving seventh and eighth graders. It was a very familiar placement for me because many of the students had gone through Fort Washington and had played a sport at one time or another in their elementary years. Even then, the sheer size of the students had me a little intimidated the first time I rolled across the campus.

I was assigned a seventh grade class where students had three periods of history, language arts, and math. There was a wide range of abilities including students taking math work that I had no idea how to start. My master teacher put me at ease when she admitted she didn't know some of the stuff they were doing either, so I immediately learned the practice of letting students excel independently.

I didn't see Mrs. Thornton stand in front and teach a lot

of lessons, but she had classroom management perfected. Her system was a well-oiled machine and the students moved efficiently from one task to the next. The way her students did the work of collecting papers and taking care of the daily business really gave me a model to use because of my own dexterity problems. Of course, they were older but everything seemed doable with elementary students.

Their ages and maturity made me believe that my approach would have to be different than what I was used to. I would be firm and professional, more like college than elementary school. I vividly remember two incidents that changed my thinking. First, this class had a clown and he wasn't very funny. Much of his humor was disrespectful and he felt he could speak freely when he wished. I loved to laugh and wanted to use my sense of humor often, but this young man did not make me laugh.

The first couple of weeks I was there, I was strictly an observer and wasn't in a position to have to resolve any conflicts. After awhile, I did small groups and built some relationships with the young folks in my charge. Finally, in the latter stages of my tenure there, I got to teach the whole class. Immediately, my young comedian friend started in and wanted to embarrass me. After asking him to stop, he made a rude remark and I used my best coaching voice while asking him to leave. The class was quiet and he just sat there. I looked at him again and repeated my request. He moved.

After the class, two of the kids that were in my groups had made me a card. They just wanted me to know they appreciated me. It was obvious they wanted me to feel OK, but I was taken by their sensitivity. The next day, they brought me these plastic turtles and wrote a note saying I was in their club.

That same weekend, I was out to dinner and ran into the

young guy whom I had removed a couple of days earlier. He watched me all night and finally made his way over to my table. He shook my hand, met my wife, and hung around as if he was waiting for something. He even brought his mom over to meet me and we had a brief, nice visit. He finally went back, but before leaving my table he put his arm around me. I nodded and patted his back so he knew I wasn't mad at him.

It was good to know that even though they were bigger, smarter, and more socially active, they were still children and wanted to give and receive assurances when things got a little too real. I really opened up more after that and had a better time. The second moment when I really knew that these were young people in need of guidance was when we shared a tragedy together. We were watching the Space Shuttle launch as Christa Mcauliffe was about to be the first teacher in space. As soon as the explosion happened, our class was silent except for two big guys in the corner who stood up, high-fived each other, and laughed as if they had won the Super Bowl. I just stared at them for what seemed like fifteen minutes and they knew they'd blown it. I learned that day that teachers had to teach kids to care.

I left Kastner and finished my year at my home school, Fort Washington. Dr. Sparks had a plan; I would be placed in my friend Erla Stanley's sixth-grade class. She'd helped me coach and we had a great relationship, so this would be fun. I would take Erla's class, teach full-time, which was the goal in the program for our last placement, and Erla would work with the office. She was leaving in June to take a promotion in our district office, and I would be her replacement. I felt fortunate as my colleagues in the university program were pounding the pavement for work and I was walking into a tailor-made situation.

Everything went like clockwork, but I was a little disappointed in the difference in the way the students treated each other during school compared to the teamwork type of environment in which I'd always seen them operate. The last straw came when a new student came and I asked two of my more athletic, popular boys to show him around and introduce him to their friends. You would have thought I'd robbed their mothers. They rolled their eyes, smacked their lips, and made this new boy feel worthless. I had noticed the class was a little spoiled, pretty immature, and really took their comfy lives for granted. When they added rude, I snapped and we had a class meeting. For the first time in my life, I spilled my guts and laid out my story for about two hours.

I told them about water skiing and intensive care. I shared the pain of having a dream and having it taken away in an instance. I told them about Coach who saved my life by filling me with hope. I explained to them about how my friends came to my rescue and were there to make my life full and complete. I spoke of losing Dale and how I missed him. And finally, I asked them to celebrate their wins in life because they had much for which to be thankful.

For the entire time, you could have heard a pin drop. They said nothing as the bell rang and they went home and, frankly, I can't honestly say I noticed any difference in them the rest of the year. I knew, though, what I wanted to bring to teaching.

Sure enough, that summer I signed my first contract and was going to earn a regular salary with full benefits. I spent the summer getting supplies, working with my wife and mom as they decorated my room, and planning lessons. Then, on a magical September morning in 1986, forty sixth-grade students marched into room number 19 at Fort Washington wide-eyed and staring at me. I was their teacher, and it was my turn to start giving back the things that I had received.

137

III

Having the Opportunity to Give Hope and Love to Others is My Life's Reward.

August, 1986

*T*he biggest games in which I ever played didn't match the tension I felt as I readied for my first day as a sixth-grade teacher. It's weird how as adults, we'd never be nervous around a twelve year old in a restaurant, on the street, in the mall, or in our homes. They would almost be in the way. On this day, though, a group of youngsters I was about to spend a year with had me totally intimidated. I prayed that they would like me and hoped they'd learn something. I fretted over everything from how to place the desks, whether to sharpen the pencils, and even what to wear. I had decorated my room with my wife and mom, but it wasn't very elaborate due to our limited artistic ability. In fact, the gal next door who was my mentor had done so much that her class looked like Disneyland compared to mine and I was a little embarrassed. Luckily, the morning bell was seconds away and my nerves made sure that things like décor were not that important. I will never forget the mist in my eyes when those forty (yes, forty) twelve year olds walked through that door and took their seats. They looked at me with excitement, nervousness, and wonder all at the same time. There was no prejudice, discrimination, or even doubt on their faces. All they knew was that I was their teacher. It remains one of the proudest moments of my life.

I had wondered many times how I would deal with the big "it." Would we talk about it or would I ignore it and see if anyone brought it up. I finally thought that if I wanted to create a family, we had to have an open and honest climate and I decided to immediately introduce the elephant in the room. After calling roll and putting names with faces, I had them fill out some information cards. After the cards were collected, I had them get comfortable so I could talk for a bit. "You may notice that I look different than other teachers you have had . . ."

For the next hour, you could hear a pin drop as I rambled on from water skiing to intensive care. They never took their eyes off of me as I explained the challenges I'd seen and they nodded their approval as I told them I'd need their help to get through the days. They laughed at my jokes and were quiet when I was serious. It was a connection and I was in love. Any doubts over the decision to teach were a distant memory.

When my talk ended I asked for questions. The students, MY students, looked around to see if anyone would break the ice and a single hand went up. I was sure I'd inspired some thought and someone would ask me to delve into my psyche, and I was prepared. Our mutual concern for human development would lead to our first learning adventure together and it was going to be profound. I can't remember who asked, but I called on the hand to share his question. "How fast does your chair go?" asked my man to the delight of his friends, "and can you pop a wheelie?" I had to show them and when my front wheels popped up, I was bombarded with "Cool!"

For the next thirty minutes, we had a question and answer session that was a blast. The more gruesome blood stories, the better the response. They particularly loved the idea that I could cut my leg wide open, bleed profusely, and not feel the pain. At that point, they decided I was "lucky." I was thinking they were right. All year long when asked how I liked teaching, all I could say was, "I'm having a great time."

I was in a conversation once, prior to starting my teaching job, where concern was addressed about my ability to teach. It was a discussion about not being able to write on the board, staple papers, or do the simple tasks teachers do every day that require dexterity. I used a special splint to write, but it didn't work with chalk, overhead projectors, and things of that nature. It was a little intimidating to think about all the things I couldn't do, so I was a little nervous on the management of my classroom.

The one thing I knew I could do, though, was build an environment where we were a family. I trusted my ability to have relationships, so I was willing to move forward in spite of a little fear. Once it got going, I knew I'd be fine. It was a matter of changing my thought process from "I can't write on the chalkboard?" to "how can I find another way to use the chalkboard." Needless to say, help was close by.

I survived as a teacher by employing the greatest work force anyone could imagine. If I needed a volunteer to write on the board, every hand would shoot up to help. Not a day went by when students didn't offer to stay in from recess to help me with something. I really felt during my first year that I would teach for free. I got more joy and satisfaction from those sixth graders than any task or project in which I'd ever been involved. It was awesome, and I thought I'd teach forever. There was, though, this constant nagging inside of me that yearned for a grand stage on which to make my statement to the world. I felt like I was constantly trying to prove the no-hopes wrong and teaching didn't end that quest. It did satisfy the itch for awhile, though.

As much as I loved coaching, I was certain that my need for some huge moment was being fed by competition, and we had our best year ever in football that first year. Our team went through the season undefeated and tied for the championship. We had a little Super Bowl with the other undefeated team. We lost, but it was great fun. I do think that I was starting to believe that I could be a successful coach and imagined myself coaching at a higher level. I even talked to some friends at the local junior high, but it didn't work out. It wasn't a big deal, though, and I knew I could stay at Fort Washington for awhile.

Teaching was tough, but I loved it so much I didn't notice. We took our sixth graders to a three-day camp in the mountains of Sonora and I wheeled through the trails and paths with them. I celebrated Christmas with my students and couldn't believe the gifts I received. I discovered that Valentine's Day was big in elementary school and parents would throw lavish parties whenever a significant event occurred. I worked with my mentor who was awesome in showing me how to use teaching strategies that would help students learn. As we got to the end, I felt as though I grew as a teacher and my students learned. I was espically pleased what I learned about community. Young people are loving and accepting, and we finished the year like a family. I wondered if we could create this kind of harmony in a room, could we teach a whole grade level about love and tolerance? Crazier yet, how about trying to run an entire school with the idea that we need to love each other as its creed. Anyway, I was in no position to try to talk about those things; I was just proud of my first year. On the last day, I told my students how much I loved them and asked them to remember our time together as a time where we all learned from each other. They walked out for the summer and I cried like a baby.

When I came back for my second year, I couldn't believe how much better I felt. The confidence of having a year under my belt was amazing. I had a sense of what would happen, and that was very comforting. My class and I had that same first day talk and we became fast friends. I was still having a great time and learning a lot, but by the middle of the year, I knew I wanted to try something else. I wasn't bored, but I wanted to try and create that same class climate at the intermediate school level. I had heard horror stories, but my student teaching taught me that those students needed love as much, or more, than younger kids.

142

I also really wanted to try and coach older athletes after working with elementary-aged sports for eight years. I had another undefeated football team, who lost again in the little Super Bowl (I was starting to think I'd never win "the big one). We did win the basketball championship that year, though". I was actually getting a reputation as a pretty good coach, so when I went over to meet the administration at Kastner Intermediate School, they were very interested. Sure enough, as the school year wound down, they had a place for me and I accepted. After eight incredible years where I learned how to coach, teach and, more importantly, learned that I could make my way in society from a wheelchair, it was time to go. Fort Washington had a nice assembly in my honor and, again, I cried like a baby.

September, 1986

*L*et's face it; I had settled into a pretty nice life. From where I'd been, things were significantly better than I had a right to expect. I had made my peace with not walking, but there were all these subtle realities that came with it that were difficult to swallow. There was the dependence on mechanical things, sudden illnesses, a million inconveniences, and the constant reminders of things I could no longer do (climb stairs, walk on the beach, and play sports, to name a few). I was pretty good at not letting those things get me down. Truth was I had a wife, career, insurance, reasonably good health, a car I could drive, and great friends. I had it going and had much for which to be thankful. There was one thing I feared I'd never have and, as I got older, knew I couldn't live without. I desperately wanted to be a father.

When I was in rehab, I was given zero encouragement on my future as a dad. My doctor was old school and when we brought the subject up, he shied away because he felt quadriplegics shouldn't be parents. I should have never let him get away with a value judgment like that, but I was sixteen and being a parent ranked behind football, girls, school, and beer on my priority list. So, I never pursued it. My body had undergone serious changes and I was pretty naïve. I had no idea what my options were other than adoption, which would have been fine. I did see a friend of mine in a chair have a baby with his wife, so I thought I'd at least ask some questions.

He put me in touch with a local fertility specialist. Michelle and I scheduled an appointment and found him to be wonderful. He gave us options and a variety of plans to investigate. Better yet, he gave us hope, and we embarked on a long journey of trial and error. We would

145

see the doctor at least monthly for tests and procedures and became experts on ovulation cycles. We were way too impatient to wait for these appointments and would buy home pregnancy tests to see if we got lucky. It was a little discouraging to see clear water every month, but we were in it for the long haul and not about ready to give up.

I was in the bedroom one September evening doing nothing in particular when Michelle asked me to check the little cup in the bathroom that had become a standard decoration over the last several months. I knew the routine and even though I'm not a big fan of body fluids, I was totally comfortable with reading the pregnancy test and trying not to sound too disappointed. I was less prepared on this night when I looked and saw blue water. I was sure my eyes were playing tricks on me and called Michelle in to look. We were borderline hysterical as we did everything possible to convince ourselves that we had made a mistake. Sure enough, the next day she went to the doctor and it was confirmed that Michelle was definitely pregnant. I was over the top.

Dickens wrote, "It was the best of times; it was the worst of times." I'm sure he wasn't thinking about the Eben family when he penned that classic line, but it pretty accurately summed up the next nine months in our house. Michelle's morning sickness lasted twenty-four hours a day, seven days a week for nine months. We couldn't drive next door without a restroom stop and she learned to find a toilet in the strangest of places. She was a tiny girl at five feet tall and one hundred ten pounds soaking wet. Michelle put on so much weight in so short of time, the doctor scolded her and she spent the last couple months on bed rest. We had hired a nursing assistant to come in and get me dressed and ready for work, so it was fine. She was just miserable.

I, on the other hand, was out of control. I was easily the most excited, obnoxious father-to-be in history. I wore

146

the shirt, the hat, and any other thing that could announce my fast-approaching fatherhood. A conversation with me wasn't complete until I shared my news. I wanted the room done, the furniture in place, clothes purchased, etc., all before the second trimester. If it were up to me, I would have had that child enrolled in college before it was born. Strangely enough, the months went fast, and Michelle and my mom came and woke me up early on the morning of May 23, 1987.

"It's time to go have a baby," my mom announced, and I was pumped. We got up and drove to the hospital for a long day of labor. Our day was a stereotype as I could do nothing right. We had attended birthing classes, but apparently I was a poor student. I couldn't rub her back right, was too slow with the ice chips, and not adept enough at the breathing exercises. I did get the epidural ordered, though, putting me back in good grace.

It was right about four in the afternoon when things got busy. I could see the baby's head and Michelle pushed for what seemed like hours. The doctor noticed the baby's heart start to race and said it was cesarean section time, so we moved to the operating room. He started to cut and within minutes, I heard the cry. I vaguely remember the doctor lifting this baby up and introducing me to my son, Jared Paul Eben. The weighing and cleaning was a blur, but when I went with the nurse to put him in his little crib, I knew I'd experienced life's greatest reward. Again, Coach Bohan got a little smarter and I had a win to celebrate that I was sure would never be topped.

I'm pretty certain that the rehab doctor who I had questioned the wisdom of quadriplegics parenting was wrong. It would be fair, though, to call it challenging and humbling. Let's face it; I wasn't a lot of help in the early days. I couldn't get up in the night when my son cried. Since I had no use of my hands, I couldn't change diapers or help dress and bathe him. My wife worked hard and bore the brunt of the responsibility. I certainly was there and offered moral support, but that was it. I carried him in a backpack type thing that I wore in the front, and I enjoyed the feeling of holding him close. I missed the little things like rolling around on the floor with him and picking him up when he learned to walk, but it was all worth it.

As Jared grew up, he learned to climb up on my lap and we were a regular pair around town. It was pretty funny actually because as he turned four and five, he would rather ride in my wheelchair than walk. I was as normal as possible. I figured out how to wedge a soft baseball in my hands and underhand pitch to him. He actually hit pretty well and played little league for a few years. I even coached his team one year when they were in a jam. One game, though, when he was about eight, he got hit by a pitch and that was the end of his baseball career.

As much of a jock as I thought I was, I knew early on that my son was not me. He loved videos and movies, and from the time he was about two, he could operate the television and VCR by himself. The dude could fix the tracking, check the wiring in the back, and fix all the connections before he was three. It got comical because I had to call him when I couldn't figure out what to do. A close friend bought him a little computer for his fourth birthday and his talents became clear. He was a technological whiz, which couldn't be more different than me. By the time he was in elementary school, Jared was the kid who walked around school fixing all the computers on campus and serving as a resource for teachers to help them connect to the network and problem-solve daily issues that arose. So, he found his niche. I worried about the time he spent playing video games and the fact that he was usually on the outside looking in when it came to making friends, but his skills would come to pay off nicely.

Where my physical limitations came into play was in the

area of discipline. He developed quite a temper, and I struggled with him. By the time he was about seven, he figured out that I wasn't able to impose my will on him at all. Jared took full advantage and learned to talk back, run away from me, and totally defy me. My wife did not believe in spanking or disciplining him, so it was up to me and it was a painful challenge. I tried to reason, I yelled and screamed, and I waited him out. I always felt that if I weren't in a wheelchair, none of that would have happened because I could have been a physical presence and he'd never challenge that. I don't think parenting is about being physical; don't get me wrong, it's just that he knew I couldn't do anything if he pushed it, so he did. As much as I loved him, when he left elementary school, I genuinely considered the idea that he and I would not be able to co-exist in the same home. My wife was willing to let him scream at her and she catered to his disrespectful tone. I couldn't take it and lost my temper many times and we came to a crossroads as he entered the seventh grade.

January, 1990

I did, in fact, leave elementary school and teach at the middle school level, which was fun. I also enjoyed the coaching at that level, but found it less thrilling than I had thought. I coached football, basketball, and track, but it wasn't hugely fulfilling. I enjoyed my time with the students and never wanted to just teach and leave at three o'clock, but I knew immediately that my future wouldn't be in jockdom. We won plenty, lost some, but my mind and heart were getting distracted, and I didn't really love it like I had hoped.

It was during my second year at Kastner Intermediate School that my future flashed before my eyes. An acquaintance of mine was a principal at one of our elementary schools and called me out of the blue. He was looking for an assistant principal and wondered if I was interested in administration. Never had I thought of myself as one of the management, but my intrigue surprised me. I found myself pondering the possibilities to put my belief system to the test on a broader level. If I could get a classroom of students to put aside peer pressure and "coolness," could I reach an entire school? I brought it up to my boss, and he surprised me even more by telling me to consider administration at Kastner, which would be looking to hire three or four entry-level management employees. I was flattered and interested. I made the decision to go for it and I landed a new job in administration. This was the beginning of a new phase in my life and was a step in the direction of whatever magic feeling I was pursuing. I still couldn't put my finger on it, but something was out there that I wanted and I was determined to find it. I couldn't wait to be a part of the leadership team. I was pumped to be in on all the big secrets, decisions, and excitement. I knew nothing of administration, but I had visions of grandeur and was ready to change the world.

I heard somewhere in my life that ninety-nine percent of the disabled population was unemployed and reliant on public assistance to survive. I had made a conscious decision early on in my life in a wheelchair to disassociate myself with the handicapped world. Mostly, I was afraid of being stereotyped, but I also thought if I worked hard and was visible, I'd do some good in changing the perception that the disabled population was not a force in the world of employment. I was somewhat proud of the fact that I had achieved a relatively uncommon level of success for someone in my physical situation. Certainly, you could look across school campuses around the country and find very few folks in wheelchairs that had completed college and were teaching and coaching. There are plenty of successful brothers and sisters in chairs out there, but many of them were in an industry related to our disability, which is cool. For absolutely no apparent reason, though, I was bound and determined to make it in the "real" or able-bodied world. That being the case, I should have been content with my life as a teacher, husband, and father. The local media ran several news stories about me, so the community was noticing me. I had made a pretty good mark before I reached my thirtieth birthday, but I wanted something more. Though I wasn't entirely sure of the destination, I was driven to chart new territory and wanted to continue to do things that no one in a wheelchair had done before. One goal I had for myself was to become a principal at a high school, but that wasn't very realistic at this point in my career. We only had three high schools and those were huge political jobs. Something of that magnitude was many years away and hardly worth thinking about. I wanted to prove, though, that I could make it in the world of leadership, and now was the time to put up or shut up.

For me to be successful, I had to answer *four really im-*

portant questions for myself. I'm probably a slow learner, but I spent the next six years bouncing around our district in a variety of jobs and schools to find the answers. Looking back, there was never a magical moment or epiphany, but I did embark on a journey where I found some truths about myself and my profession. I can see now that my trek was a mission to discover if I could be a leader. I never thought I was going to be a story on the level of Franklin Roosevelt, but I did feel a little like I was carrying a burden to prove that people from all walks of life could achieve any dream they wanted, no matter how uncommon or unlikely. The *first question* would set the tone: *Would I be able to find satisfaction and fulfillment without being in the classroom?* What a bummer it would be to have this grand plan derailed because of the simple fact that I was unhappy. Well, I got off to a rocky start, at best.

I was sure I'd be in the middle of cutting edge discussions and decisions, but boy was I disappointed. There was no secret handshake or initiation, no manual with administration codes that let me in on the big party that teachers thought the management team celebrated every day. To my disappointment, it appeared early on that this new job was just more work for the same pay, and I was ticked. I would spend every day from about eleven in the morning until two in the afternoon patrolling the grounds during our three lunch periods. The excitement of telling students every day to take their sodas inside the cafeteria was inspiring, but not why I ventured into education. In short, I seriously regretted my decision.

To make matters worse, the only contact I had with students was negative. After spending four years building positive relationships with young people, I spent my day disciplining kids and actually kicking them out of school. Every student I came across left my office suspended, with detention, or assigned to Saturday School. I certainly went into an immediate funk because I wasn't

153

making a difference. The more repeat customers, the less productive I felt. I was blown away by the reality that I couldn't turn some of these young folks around and was very discouraged. I was pretty sure my move to the big time would be short lived, but I got a glimmer of hope during the early part of that first year.

Our district decided to open a new high school the following fall and named the principal, a guy with whom I had a good but casual relationship. Somewhere in a conversation, he broached the prospect of me helping him open the new school, a thought that was intriguing. In thinking about where I could help the most, I latched on to the idea that I would be a really good athletic director. I was sure I had the answer to my professional pursuit of happiness. I would be out of the negative stuff and surrounded by the thing I loved the most; sports. It was a natural fit and the new principal was encouraging. I'll never forget his words at an event we both attended. He said, "It is not IF you will be my athletic director . . . you WILL BE my athletic director." I hung onto those words throughout that difficult first year and made my plans to move to the new school. The negativity was temporary now, so I knew I could survive. I started studying athletic directors and spent some time with my father, who was the athletic director at Arroyo Grande High School on the Central Coast. As the time came to start the transition, I was ready and excited. There would be an interview process, but I knew that was a formality because the principal and I had a secret agreement . . . or so I thought.

I interviewed in the early spring and knew that I had nailed the questions. I felt great and knew that I had found my life's calling. Since I was an elementary and intermediate school guy, people were surprised when I made the final two for the job. High school athletics is very important in our area and the fraternity is a pretty close-knit group, so my name wasn't bantered about in all the speculation. I, of course, knew because the principal and I had a secret agreement that was about to come true. Soon, I would be on the ground floor of building an entire program and was very excited. I waited for the call and it took longer than I thought. Days turned to weeks and I never got my inevitable confirmation. I heard the rumors that the other finalist, a very successful volleyball coach in our community, was going to get the job, but I wasn't concerned. After all, the principal and I had a secret agreement, didn't we?

I learned a lot about such agreements that May. After a long period of no news, the principal called me and told me that I had lost out on the job. He didn't mention any deals or agreements, just thanked me and hung up. He did offer to meet with me and even arranged a date and time. I was so stunned, though I didn't know what to say or do. I was humiliated, angry, and felt betrayed. More relevant, though, was the realization that I didn't know what I was going to do. Graciously, I was given the chance to stay where I was and everyone was very supportive. All of my colleagues knew how disappointed I was and did everything possible to ease the pain. The offer to keep my job helped, but I was feeling my first real professional failure and it was painful. Another problem with my current job was that I was miserable and knew another year of supervision and discipline would ruin me forever. In a daze, I kept my appointment with the principal of the new school.

We met at the construction site that in a matter of a couple of months would become the Buchanan Educational Center. I was really mad at this guy, but I was polite and moderately interested in what he had to say. Surprisingly, he offered no apology or even an explanation of what I felt was months of deceit and, ultimately, betrayal. In fact, he had the audacity to tell me he still wanted me on his team, albeit in a role very similar to the current job in which I was struggling. I explained my discontent and even went as far as to claim complete lack of interest in administration as my career path. He cautioned me to be patient and give educational leadership a chance. He was selling the opening of a new school as a chance to grow and be on the ground floor of an exciting project, and I bought it hook, line, and sinker. I made the change but was going to give it one year. If I couldn't positively answer my most basic question of being happy by the end of the second year, I was going back into the classroom. One thing for sure, though, my competitive juices were in full flow and I was going over to that new school to prove to that certain principal that he made the mistake of his life.

August, 1990

We open school every fall in our area with temperatures well over one hundred degrees and this fall was no exception. Amazingly, our new school opened for our students and we were not close to ready. We had no bathrooms, cafeteria, library, and, worst of all, air conditioning. Every day was a challenge just to survive in the heat. By the afternoon, we were all soaking wet with sweat and with water from dousing ourselves. Our challenge as the leadership team was to keep people positive and that was an incredible lesson in mind over matter. We brought in portable restrooms and sack lunches to solve those problems, but there was no answer for the heat. We all suffered, but our administrators agreed not to let our kids and teachers see it on our faces. For me, I could have made a good excuse to stay home, as the heat was dangerous for me. I knew, though, that if I kept a wet towel around my neck I'd survive. I also knew if I could keep a positive attitude, others would follow. They couldn't have been more miserable than I was at the time, and if I wasn't complaining they better not complain. In what was probably the worst condition I had seen or probably ever would see in education, I found fulfillment. For the first time, I saw potential in this thing called leadership. I still performed mundane and unpleasant tasks, but I had a chance to step out and try to influence people. It started with trying to be a role model in a trying situation.

Soon, though, it grew. I was in daily conversations about trying to find a new way to educate students. I found out that I had ideas to share and relished the chance to talk and debate. I also found out that I wanted to be in the middle of the action. As the year went on, I'd get angry if I was excluded from the discussions and went toe to toe with the principal more than once about being included. I was starting to really care about my place in the organization and started jockeying for position at the table. I wanted my opinions to be heard and I wanted to move our new school forward. Somewhere in the midst of this excitement, I forgot about going back into the classroom. I was energized, even intoxicated, by the big picture of a school. I was still coaching basketball, but started to see that it was getting in the way; a huge step because I always envisioned myself in coaching like my father. The year prior, I had decided to stop coaching football after spending a season where I had to sit in the emergency room with three different players for broken bones. Our team had endured a rough season because we were placed in a league where my seventh graders played against eighth graders. We went into every game just hoping to survive and not get kids injured. It really made me question myself on whether or not my future rested in athletics. The last trip to the hospital with one of my players made me realize that I didn't love coaching anymore. This was the time for a clean break. I found myself not wanting to miss meetings for practice or games, and by the end of the season, I knew my jock days, at least as a coach, were over.

January, 1991

*D*uring this time of growth and self-discovery, God showed Michelle and me that He had a sense of humor. One Saturday night, we went to dinner before a Fresno State basketball game. We were season ticket holders and never missed. Sometimes we took Jared, who was barely three, but on this night we left him with a sitter. My wife was in her senior year of college and would soon graduate with her degree in accounting. Always the money saver, I was surprised she wanted to go to Niccola's Restaurant, a pretty swanky, expensive place. I ordered a good bottle of wine and was ticked when she wouldn't drink any with me. Somewhere around dessert, she explained her lack of consumption; she was pregnant with our second child. I was shocked, but the excitement took over and I was ready to celebrate. I was working a lot, but the pregnancy was smooth and the months passed quickly. I had a friend who was sort of a mess and he moved in with us to do my care. He had just gotten out of jail on some drug and alcohol charges and we wanted to help him. At the same time, he was helping us out, so it was a good thing. Anyway, since we had the boy, we decided to find out the sex of this child to see if we needed to redecorate or recycle. We did the ultrasound and left the doctor in search of frilly pink clothing. Sure enough, on October 2, 1991, Noelle Nicole Eben entered our lives. Her brother couldn't believe this little girl came out of Mom's belly. I couldn't believe I was about to raise a daughter. I prayed that God would forgive me for every inappropriate thought or action I had committed with any girl in my past. For the record, her birth date came fourteen years to the day after that water-skiing trip in high school changed my world. Coach used to say we can find wins anywhere if we look hard enough. When the darkest day of my existence turned into one of the greatest days in my life, I was pretty convinced he was right.

I proceeded to break every rule in parenting with this little girl. Make no mistake, I met my match. She had me wrapped around her very little finger from the day she was born. I set equality back several years with this child. While I raised my son to be independent and strong-willed, I would love for her to be Daddy's Little Girl forever. Like I did with Jared, I cuddled and sang to her every chance I got. I would lie in bed and snuggle up with her every night, and it was awesome. The difference with Noelle was I never wanted her to grow out of it. I fell into the trap of wanting Jared to be "all boy" and I was bound and determined to make sure Noelle would always be my baby. I could make her laugh and get her to stop crying. She would wait for me to come home from work and climb up on my lap when I arrived. It was awesome, but I knew it wouldn't be like that forever. She would grow up into a young lady and I would have to let her go . . . I'm still waiting for that to happen.

With two young children and Michelle home parenting, the increase in salary was important. I had been taking classes and earned my Master's Degree in Educational Administration around the time Noelle was born. So, my commitment to my growing family meant that I'd be in administration for the long haul.

April, 1992

*T*he *second question* I needed to answer for myself
struck a chord to any insecurities I felt about my physical situation. Simply put: *Would I be able to get kids to
listen to me in the larger environment?* I was totally
confident in the classroom, but I had control. I spent
nine months with kids and we all knew each other, so
it wasn't the same. In management, I had to help keep
the campus safe. It involved crowd control, breaking up
fights, and holding kids accountable that were not necessarily students that I knew. In fact, the kids I saw the
most now were often pretty turned off to education and
not really interested in anybody's opinion on our campus.
I certainly wasn't sure they'd respond to me.

That first year, I built a great relationship with a young
man who was arguably the toughest cat in school. He
struck fear in the heart of everyone and kids wouldn't rat
him out if he were the last guy on the face of the earth because of their concern for retaliation. Little did they know
that he and I had bonded, and he would tell me anything
I wanted to know about the people and problems out on
campus. There was a scary moment with him in the first
month, though, that I'll never forget. I was out on the pe-
rimeter of our campus doing part of my daily supervision
marathon when I turned a corner and came upon two
good-sized boys rolling around on the ground beating the
crap out of each other. They were screaming, swearing
and bloody, and I was the only one even close. I'd never
been the person to break up a fight, and I could feel the
oxygen leaving my brain as I approached. I was afraid of
helplessness. I had to stop these two before one of them
got seriously injured. I didn't know if I could get the job
done because I couldn't physically pull them apart. This
was a huge moment. If I couldn't keep the basic

campus order, I was not a credible administrator. News would travel quickly that I couldn't handle certain duties because of my disability, which for me would end any thoughts about being a real leader. I had no choice but to go for it. I literally wheeled my chair into the mess so my tires were in between their arms, not touching them, just acting like a wall between them. I yelled, "That's enough!" One of the fighters was my guy.

Right then, those two boys gave me a gift that I'll never forget; they stopped. Both guys scrambled to their feet and started blaming each other. I asked them if they were hurt and we walked together to the office. I was scared to death the whole time that they would tear after each other again, but they didn't. I was lucky because if they wanted to keep fighting there wasn't much I could do to stop them. Part of me thought, however, that it wasn't luck that stopped that fight. I had a relationship with that kid and he did what I asked of him. I remember that day thinking that maybe I could do this job. Perhaps every student just wants to be heard and respected. By reaching out to them, they would allow me to lead them. It was a lesson on which I hung my hat in the world of student discipline. At the very least, I knew I could contribute without being able to use brute strength and force.

I found myself in many situations like that over the years and have always managed to restore order. There was one moment in my second year that reminded me of the risks involved every time we step in the middle of a fight. Two boys were jawing at each other and ended up nose to nose. As is the case every time this happens on a campus, an enormous crowd gathered making a peaceful resolution almost impossible. Kids love to watch a fight and the combatants, at some point, can't walk away and still keep their dignity. So, in this case, it was on. Since I was the first one on the scene, I managed to maneuver through the crowd and squeeze myself in between the two boys. No blows had been thrown so I had time to stop the fracas before it got ugly. One of the guys was from a local group home and had a criminal past. I knew him pretty well, and drew no comfort from my association with him. Sure enough, he didn't flinch when I asked him to walk away. The other boy was less angry, but he wasn't moving either. The two kept talking to each other and questioning who would throw the first blow. I continued to ask them to walk away, but to no avail. I was pretty sure I was in trouble when one of the other counselors grabbed her student by the arm and he left. I let out a sigh of relief, but realized that I had to make sure that they both knew their defiance was unacceptable. I got my boy from the group home and sat him in my office. I asked him why he wouldn't walk away when I asked and he let me know he intended to hurt the other guy in this disturbance. Finally, I called our campus police officer who placed him under arrest for the threats. In the process, the officer searched him, pulling a large hunting knife out of his jeans that would have done serious damage. Even though that situation didn't end as easily as the other, I thought I did my job. One, my presence kept it from getting really out of hand. Second, I held the students both accountable for their actions. That simple fact solidified my belief in myself in this issue. I couldn't be a hero and keep everyone from harm's way. Sometimes, stuff happens and no matter how hard we try, we don't prevent kids from creating a mess. By making sure they pay the consequences, we still protect our kids and I don't need to be Hercules to uphold the policies of school.

I was surprised to find out that there were so many fights at school. I had not noticed violence when I taught, but it shaped a large part of my day as an administrator. I was learning that our community was pretty diverse and cultures were battling each other. Gangs were on the rise and we were constantly working to keep the gang issues out of our schools. I wasn't sure if this phenomenon was growing because of the media, poverty, or some other force, but I knew I had a responsibility to help keep kids safe in the face of so many daily acts of violence. It seemed, too, that we needed to spend some time teaching our young kids how to better get along, but we didn't.

I knew I had become credible as a keeper of the peace in the eyes of my colleagues during another fight that broke out on campus. It wasn't in my area, so I hadn't seen it start. It was during lunch and a few of our teachers were returning to class and happened on the scene. One young teacher/coach was in that group and panicked. Now, he was about six feet four inches tall and could have stopped this fight by just getting close. Instead, he ran over to me and said, "There is a fight over there and I need your help!" After we got everybody calmed down the irony of the moment struck. This big, burly jock had to come get the guy in the wheelchair to break up a fight. It was actually a nice moment because I knew that I had a role on campus and was totally accepted in that role, regardless of what I looked like. I had answered question number two, but I also know that each incident holds risks and needs to be handled with care.

April, 1993

By the time I was in my third year in management, I was getting a reputation for being pretty good with kids and was thoroughly enjoying myself. The Chamber of Commerce in my community even recognized me at their annual Hall of Fame gala as Clovis' Most Inspirational Citizen. I had gained respect as an educator who got the most out of students and established relationships with any and all types of kids. Being around young people made me happy, and as I moved into my thirties, they kept me a teenager at heart. I wasn't satisfied, though, and my journey was getting more serious. I successfully applied for a job as a Learning Director (many districts call them assistant principals) and went to work at Clovis High School, my alma mater. My principal was a guy named Steve Weil, one of the very few people in our town that I didn't know. This would become a significant relationship in my life, but at first I was pretty uncomfortable. To make things stranger, some of the teachers that I was to lead were actually faculty members when I was a student. So, with only four years of my own teaching experience, I went into the job with **another question** for which I had to come to terms: **Would I be able to effectively lead teachers who had a lot more expertise than I and, worse, still saw me as a kid?**

I rationalized the second part of that question by telling myself that the staff would get over it. In fact, it never was an issue. We had fun with the whole former student thing and I found it more helpful than anything else. I rolled around the campus for the first couple of weeks and waited for the magic cloud of leadership to rain all this knowledge on me and, surprisingly, it never came. I was fine with the kids but a little lost at where to begin with the adults. I finally started talking to the staff, just

165

asking them to tell me about their jobs. That lead to a discussion of common purpose (sort of a "Why are we teaching high school English?" sort of thing) and we were off and running. I discovered that by being honest about knowing less than them and asking the teachers to teach me about their craft, I was accepted as their leader. In fact, we got moving on some ground-breaking conversation about teaching that had great potential to solidify our curriculum. Unfortunately, I didn't get to stay long enough to see that work come to fruition.

In less than a year, my boss Steve had become my friend and mentor. He really allowed me the freedom to be myself and trusted our staff to bring me along. It really created harmony and I was enjoying the new responsibility of leading adults. Also, for the first time, my wheelchair was never a factor. I had reached a point where the only way to survive was to be successful. The days of being a token or a feel-good story were over. It was all about production, and I was getting good results in a short time. So, when Steve got promoted to the role of Area Superintendent in charge of a high school, junior high, and six elementary schools, he asked me to join him. It meant moving to another school on the other side of town, but my early years were in the Clovis West area, so it was a homecoming for me. The new high school was where many of my former students were now young juniors and seniors and it was a thrill to reconnect with them.

Steve made me the Deputy Principal at Clovis West High School, an academic and athletic power in California education. In fact, the year I arrived, the school had been named the state's Athletic High School of the Year. So, I came into a buzz saw that was doing fine without any help from me. In my new role, I was second in command of this very proud organization and had to prove myself as a community leader. By now, I loved the high school scene and wanted a chance to run one myself. This job would be the critical test of my ability and I still was new at the leading of adults. With all their success, I knew I couldn't come in and tell them much, so I searched for my role. The good news of my early days at CW was spending my time out amongst the students. The kids who knew me were glad to see a familiar face, and the students I didn't know appreciated the fact that I was out on campus hanging with them. I started going to as many events as I could and heard a lot of positive feedback about being visible.

Strangely enough, much of the positive feedback I received was from the staff. The new principal that I served was a very cool Italian dude named Gary Giannoni. We developed a great partnership and became close. He was a classic. He spent more money on one suit than I had in my whole closet. I was usually disheveled and very casual. He was immaculate and always dressed to the hilt. We shared a love of kids, though, and did our best to be everywhere. What we got was a lot of thanks from our staff and parents. Word spread quickly that we cared, and that brought us acceptance and even a warm welcome. I was in heaven. Everything seemed to be on a grand stage and our kids won everything, so I was just giddy. I noticed, though, that almost everyone in our community seemed bored with success. There wasn't a lot of joy in our successes; it was expected and routine. That was a revelation that was hard to accept, and after some thought, I found my role. I would become the school's official cheerleader and try to get everyone to enjoy the incredible work that they did every day.

I was everywhere. I went to every game, concert, play, etc. Wherever our kids and staff were, you would find Gary and me. I was out at break, lunch, before and after school, in the parking lots, it didn't matter. During class, I made friends with the secretaries, custodians, food service staff, and anyone else who walked on campus. I talked incessantly about how awesome everyone was and was sincere. I had never been around this much success and wanted everyone to be excited. Gary and I would sing stupid songs at rallies and let our kids get a little rowdy at games. Once, when we played for the section basketball title, he told the students I would shave my head if we won. We did and my hair came off. School was fun and the staff had bought in to us as leaders. I knew I had found my calling and couldn't wait to be the principal of my own school.

The last thing in my plan was something that happened by accident. Our school had morning announcements that were taped, and one day, the tape broke. There were a couple of events that wanted attention, so I was summoned to read the announcements live on the school's public address system. I don't remember the specifics, but I borrowed Robin Williams' bit and screamed loudly into the mike, "Gooooood Morning Clovis West!" I made a scene and after every event I announced, I used the line, "It will be huge!" That became my mantra and what started as a little fill-in became a daily routine for which I was best remembered. People rarely talked about the twelve to fourteen hours a day I worked or the complaints I handled. The principal and I really reshaped the school's finances and organized a parent body to help provide financial security that still is in operation. Nope, I was the morning announcement guy, and my three years at CW will always be marked by that bit of goofiness. I felt successful there and I think the three years I spent made a huge difference in my life.

Toward the end though, I was getting tired. I was keeping an impossible pace. Michelle and I would rise at four thirty each morning and I'd come home after ten at night. After events, my colleagues and I would go out for drinks and it seemed I never saw my wife. As my career flourished, my marriage was falling apart. We had been together twelve years and I felt totally disconnected. I decided to move out thinking that I wanted freedom and wasn't interested in being married anymore. I moved into

168

my mother's house and had the children part time. What I thought would never happen was happening, but the worst was yet to come. The guilt I felt for walking out on my wife got worse every day. She had given herself up for me, done my medical care, supported us financially when I was sick, and I was walking away. I broke Michelle's heart and before long it was more than I could bear.

I spent six months apart from my family. I saw the kids as often as possible, but I hated not being there to tuck them in at night. I was learning a valuable lesson about choosing work over your loved ones and started to really regret my decision. Finally, I went on a trip to Disney World to supervise our cheerleaders as they competed in a national competition. As I toured the theme parks with our girls, I was totally bummed to be in that environment without my family. I knew what I had to do, and hurried back to the hotel on the second night of our trip to find a phone. Michelle answered and I wasted no time.

"I really miss you." I said, my voice breaking from emotion, "I want to put our family back together."

She said very little, but when I returned home, we agreed to give ourselves another try. Michelle was glad, but a little reserved. I had really hurt her and she didn't feel close to me or trust me. It would take time to re-build, but my priorities were in place.

March, 1996

*T*hrough the mess in my personal life, my friend and boss Steve was very supportive of me. I needed a change in my environment to focus on my family and he understood. In fact, he began a conversation with me before we went to Florida with the cheerleaders about learning how to be THE leader of a school and I sensed he had something on his mind. Coincidentally, Steve was traveling with us to watch his daughter, a member of our cheer squad. I finally asked him if he had something on his mind, and he said he needed my help and would fill me in when we got there. I started to sense that something was wrong, and when we got to Orlando, Steve wanted to meet at, of all places, Hooters Restaurant.

We ate and hung out, and he finally spoke up. He said he was having trouble at a couple of his elementary schools and needed to make a couple of moves. He explained that the principal at one was leaving and he was worried about the morale. He asked if I was interested in becoming an elementary principal. I wasn't, but I wanted to help him out since he'd been good to me. It had to be a sign when I asked him which school I would lead. When the words "Fort Washington" fell off his lips, I knew it was my destiny. I was going back to the place were I fell in love with education and my heart needed a restart. So, right there in Hooters, I got my first principalship. I had mixed emotions, but I certainly felt like I had been given a big win.

There was about two months left of school and the transition in the job started. Since Fort was right across the street from Clovis West, I could run over and do things if needed. Mostly though, I was moving at the end of the year. As excited as I was, I was sad to leave Clovis West. I didn't want to leave the high school, but it was

171

for the best. Michelle and I had gotten back together, and I needed to work hours that gave me a family life. So, I was at peace even if I was a little depressed about saying goodbye to my work at the high school. My work, though, wasn't quite finished and two young men were about to teach me a lesson that would serve me well as a leader.

I had coached a young man named John Adams in junior high school. He was a good basketball player, but also a leader and scholar. By the time he was a senior, he was our student body president, an advanced placement scholar, and varsity athlete. Unfortunately, John had been battling illness his senior season and couldn't play. He was, however, very involved and universally respected. Late April, his illness took a turn and he needed surgery in the Bay Area. During the operation, something went tragically wrong, and we came to work on a Monday morning to hear that he lay in a coma in grave condition, surrounded by his family and friends. It appeared that John was going to die, and all we could do was wait for the call. Our campus was in shock and we prepared our crisis team. I used the morning announcements to keep the students and staff up to date, but we all were sad and feared the inevitable.

On a Wednesday, a senior All-American swimmer and water polo player who had received a scholarship to play for UC Irvine walked into my office. Dan Klatt was one of the most popular kids on campus and was one of John's close friends. Throughout his high school years, he had earned my respect. So, when he spoke, I listened. He told me he wanted to do something to change the mood at school. He felt we could energize the students by organizing a fundraiser to help John's family with their mounting hotel and food costs while they sat at their son's bedside. I only slightly chuckled when he suggested a car wash for the coming weekend. Since those generate around a hundred dollars on a good day, I figured he wouldn't help the family much. His heart, though, was in the right place and I told him I'd support him and supervise the two days. He made a pretty basic flyer and was on his way. Dan said he was pre-selling tickets for five bucks and would make money. I was really proud of him, but didn't exactly figure we'd break the bank. Oh, was I foolish.

Dan showed up that night at a volleyball game and went through the small crowd soliciting donors. We violated every policy in regards to fundraising, but I was sure we'd be forgiven. The crowd was very receptive and he did pretty well, so I started to think he'd be OK. The next day was Thursday and no less than a dozen seniors came by to get flyers for Saturday and Sunday's event. I could feel a buzz on campus and knew something strange was happening. I became car wash headquarters, and by Friday we were besieged by students, teachers, and the press who wanted to help. We had a bonafide spectacle and about one hundred of us showed up Saturday morning ready for business.

The parents of one of our senior girls owned a local car wash and her folks gave us supplies. By nine in the morning, it was raging hot, but as the day progressed, our numbers of student workers easily doubled. In one of the most unbelievable scenes I ever witnessed, our low budget operation washed over 1,000 cars in two days. The lines stretched for hundreds of yards and we were washing cars in rows three and four cars deep. By the time we finished Sunday night, we were exhausted, sunburned, and overwhelmed. We counted the money and raised almost seven thousand dollars! I looked at Dan and said through tears, "Do you realize what you've just done?"

He just smiled and answered, "This feels good."

The story was completed when John awoke from his coma and started to heal. By graduation, he was well enough to be transferred to Fresno for his rehabilitation. In a

Hollywood moment, John came to our graduation in cap and gown and was wheeled to the stage. It was the president's job to announce the entry of the graduates, and our president fulfilled his responsibility. As I sat there during graduation which was my last duty at CW, I knew I'd witnessed a miracle. John continues to prosper to this day.

As for Dan, he would become a college All-American and represent our country in the Athens Olympic Games in water polo. I was reading his clippings during his Olympic experience and someone asked him about his proudest or favorite memory. He answered with his story about the car wash, and I smiled. It was easily the finest thing I'd seen a young person do for a friend in my life. He did something for me, too, that was less obvious. In fact, he taught me a valuable leadership lesson during that week. Dan made me remember the importance of being in a community where its citizens take care of each other. To be a real leader, you must be willing to put aside your own stuff for the good of others and inspire everybody to do the same. This young man believed that he could do something more important than win medals, and he earned the total respect of everyone at our school and in our community. Dan literally changed people's lives by acting on his simple belief system. Thankfully, my education came just in time. A few short weeks after the car wash, I walked across the street to MY school. It was time for me to be the leader. I only had *one more question* to answer: *What did I believe?*

August, 1996

*T*o be honest, being the boss was kind of cool on several levels. First, at thirty-six years old, I was the youngest principal in our district, and I was pleased at the fact that I'd earned the trust of my superintendent and our board. Second, deep down where I never let people see, I knew I proved the doubters wrong. So many days in rehab were spent trying to be counseled on the limited possibilities that I was facing as a sixteen-year-old quadriplegic with a future that included a wheelchair. Most of what I heard was about how to survive or get by. Never did I hear how to succeed or even become a leader. Coach always told me that I "wouldn't let the no-hopes win" and his message was making sense. There was also a twisted little irony about the turn of events that made me smile. I remembered being a teenaged basketball coach who rolled out to this school one day with long hair and an earring. To think that goofball would one day be the principal of that place in the ultra-conservative district in which we lived was good stuff. In truth, though, I was filled with a sense of accomplishment and personal satisfaction, but I didn't ever share it. I would be lying, though, if I didn't admit to feeling good about what I had done with my life.

It wasn't long, though, before I noticed how different the hot seat felt compared to the other support roles in which I worked. I slept a little worse, my level of concern was much higher, and I knew there weren't many places to turn to for guidance. All of a sudden, it was my deal and I was responsible for every decision and issue that came out of Fort Washington. I've never been one to be afraid, but the accountability of this gig definitely had my attention. I had done a little homework on the state of the staff and community and knew that there were a couple issues that had been left unresolved. Starting there, I made a couple of immediate decisions that helped me be someone that everyone saw as a leader. I also went to every class-room and talked to the kids about why I looked different than most other folks they encountered in school. As I expected, they liked the story and were more interested in how fast my chair could go than any social commentary. So, I felt very welcome at my new home and my principal-ship got off to a good start. It had been awhile since I'd been around the younger children, but any anxiety was immediately replaced by their unabashed and genuine love they showed me every day. If ever I needed an ego boost or emotional pick-me-up, I was in the right place.

Two things happened right off the bat that really enriched my experience and helped me be successful. First, as I went into the fall of my first year, my daughter Noelle was entering kindergarten. Though we lived in a different neighborhood, I enrolled her at Fort and we were able to spend our days together. It was very cool and, in a way, gave me some common ground with our parent commu-nity. My son Jared was entering fourth grade and was very content at his current school. Since we had been through a lot of heartache as a family in recent months, we chose to leave him where he was happy. The second thing was a surprise to me. One of the first tasks I had to accomplish was to hire a secretary. I had been fortunate to walk into my previous jobs where the position was al-ready filled. I considered myself extremely lucky to inher-it professional women who were beyond helpful, but I was ready to hire someone who might be with me for the long term. In fact, one of the reasons I accepted the job was the knowledge that I'd get to bring my own staff into the office. I really had no one in mind and looked forward to interviewing. One day in that initial summer, (during and after the CW graduation, I had a few weeks with the Fort staff and community before we broke for vacation) one of the existing office staff came in and closed the door. She was pretty quiet but very professional and had a reputation as a competent worker. Cathy Morse was as conservative as I was funky, but she worked up the nerve to come in and express her interest in being my right hand.

"Mr. Eben," she said really nervously, "if you don't have anyone in mind, I'd love to be your office manager."

She was so serious it made me chuckle. I stammered something about being interested and encouraged her to interview for the job. Sure enough, after the interview process, she was selected and we began a relationship that has been a critical part of my life and continues to this day.

I found the job to be a little bit of a roller coaster ride. There were great days and tough days, but I quickly discovered that success at this level of work was not beyond my reach. I needed to be able to survive the ride, but I wasn't worried about that. I found myself able to make decisions. I wasn't afraid of making mistakes and made plenty, but nothing that couldn't be fixed. I was gaining confidence in my ability to do the work, but I was being nagged by something more. I didn't want to just survive the job; I wanted to make a difference. People come and go in the workplace, and our business is no exception. We come to a school, work hard, and move on. We judge our success by how well we do the work, and there is nothing wrong with that. I wanted to do something more, though. I wanted to make an impact that would last after I left. By focusing on only the work, I wouldn't accomplish my goal. My sense was I had to change the culture to, even in a small way, reflect my belief system and be something that would last. I went back to the one question that I had yet to answer for myself: What do I believe is important for school, or life for that matter? To really matter in the history of this great school, I needed to answer that query and do something about it.

In the meantime, I had heard that confidence and morale was low, and I was trying to help. Being a decision maker was helpful for our parents. They were a successful bunch in their lives and demanded quality for their children. They pushed hard and that is a challenge for educators. I embraced the parents and made them partners in the school. I immediately put them to work with me on a technology plan that had been lacking, according to parent surveys. The obvious benefit was the increase in the computers and printers that became available for teachers and students to use. The secondary benefit was the development of a mutual trust between the staff and our community. We wanted the same things and could work together. Really, these parents were like anyone else and wanted someone to care about their children. The difference with this group was they had the time, resources, and initiative to make things happen. The school could embrace that fact or resist it, which was hurtful. There seemed to be a little resistance when I came, but we got through that and developed good relationships. The more we talked about the kids, and the more time I spent cheerleading for and with their kids, the more we agreed and things continued to get better.

The staff reminded me a little of my previous experience at Clovis West. They were about as talented a group with whom I'd ever hoped to work, but they were a little ho-hum about their accomplishments. They, too, had a lot of which to be proud and didn't seem to be enjoying themselves. I had heard that the teachers felt like the parents were out of control and the administration was not supporting the work of the staff. I didn't see that, but there was clearly an attitude that people worked in isolation and didn't spend any time team building. So, I tried to make it fun. We formed a faculty band and played at a rally for our students and at a community concert. That ended up being really fun and helped us bond. We started socializing together and even put on a staff talent show for our annual school carnival. It became an annual event and we would always try to outdo each other by having the best dance or song. Besides us having a great time, our community loved it and we attracted a pretty large audience for the show each year. For me anyway, the key was we really started to enjoy each other. At one point, we got so carried away that several of us left our Christmas party and went out and got tattoos; a very proud moment. We had been exchanging gifts and drinking margaritas when the party wound down. One of our teachers yelled out, "I want to go get a tattoo!"

Within minutes, members of our staff started challenging each other with "if you get one, I'll get one" kind of talk. Finally, I announced, "I want a tattoo, let's go!"

We loaded into three vehicles and drove about fifteen minutes to downtown Fresno to a small tattoo parlor. One by one, we went in and did the deed. I had my children's initials forever imprinted on my arm. Teachers had flowers, butterflies, and other artwork tattooed on places that hopefully few will see. Oddly, some of the ladies that are now branded are teachers that no one would expect to see at a tattoo parlor. Now, we were bonded for life whether we liked it or not. One of our staff members told me later that we had built a family during that time, and that meant a lot to me. The fun times allowed us to tackle the difficult things and moved Fort out of its comfort zone. We learned not to settle for doing well, we wanted our kids to be the best they could be, so we raised our expectations of ourselves. It took some time to get there, but we were friends and felt safe.

October, 1997

*L*ife continued to get in the way of all my good times. During my second year, I broke out into a cold sweat that never went away. By the end of the day, I would be soaking wet with large beads of sweat pouring off of me. I would be at work wrapped in towels looking like I had just finished a fifteen-round boxing match. After twenty years of being pretty free of the health problems associated with quadriplegia, I was in a full-blown crisis that wouldn't go away. It really had started a year earlier but I chalked it up to a bladder infection and treated it with antibiotics. It kept reappearing and though I was frustrated, I wasn't overly concerned.

Eventually, my condition was affecting my work for the first time. I was trying to find solutions and spent a lot of time at the doctor's office trying to find the answer to the sweating, which after a year was becoming unbearable. The sweating in my body is an indicator of pain. I can't feel pain below my chest, but if something happens to me on a part of my body that is paralyzed, the sweat warns me that something is wrong. During this period, I knew it was my bladder because I had a constant urinary infection and the sweating went away when I treated the problem. Relief, however, never lasted more than a day, and we couldn't figure it out. My doctor even performed surgery twice to get my bladder to empty, but nothing worked. These surgeries cut my urethra to clear the way for my bladder to empty. It was a costly procedure because it took away my ability to have an erection, ending my sexual intercourse days. When my bladder still wouldn't empty, I was discouraged and faced the possibility that this problem would last awhile. Thankfully, he sent me to Los Angeles to see a specialist who confirmed that my bladder wasn't emptying correctly. The difference was, though, he seemed to know why. It seemed my bladder itself was infected and any urine inside of it caused great pain, which resulted in my sweats. There was a solution and it was drastic. I had to be cut completely open, have my bladder removed and replaced by a rebuilt organ made out of intestine. It would fix the problem but not without some consequences. The surgery was difficult and I would be hospitalized for three weeks. I would have to have a hole cut into my side called a stoma. For the rest of my life, I would have to insert a catheter or tube into the stoma every few hours to drain the urine. For years, I had been able to urinate on my own, so this new dependence on a catheter and someone to perform the procedure a few times a day was tough to take. Unfortunately, there was no decision to make. I couldn't continue to live with the chills and sweats, so I decided to tough it out until summer and go for the operation during my vacation.

June, 1998

The operation would happen in the city of Orange, California, next to Anaheim. You could see Disneyland and Angel Stadium from my window, but I never got to look. From the moment I arrived, things didn't go well. First, the hospital didn't have me registered and I sat in the waiting room until they contacted the doctor. This took three hours and I was pretty agitated.

Somewhere in this time, I was visited by an administrator who was getting my billing information. As he got close to the end of his form, he announced, "and this isn't covered by your insurance so we'll be billing you personally." I almost passed out and Michelle started to cry. As I was just about to cancel everything and run out the door, I made a phone call to our school district's benefits staff.

"I'm down in the UC Irvine hospital having surgery in a few hours," I said panicked, "and they just told me the surgery isn't covered!"

Mercifully, the voice on the other end told me there was a mistake and got everything taken care of quickly. We were good to go. I went into the operating room for a three hour procedure. Twelve hours later I was finished. I awoke and was totally delirious. My mom said something to me about being on the table for twelve hours, but I didn't care. I just wanted more morphine to sleep. Apparently, the doctor found a host of other problems and I came out with more than a new bladder. He found my stomach to be a mess and needed to reconstruct my bowel tract. He told me that my recovery would take a month for each hour I was on the table and he was right.

Michelle had to go home to work and take care of our

kids, so I spent three long weeks with my brother Scott there holding my hand. I ate out of a tube and laid there day after day until my body and systems started functioning again. When I was released, I even stayed an extra week at Scott's house in Los Angeles before I was up for a four-hour ride back to Clovis. Michelle came and took me home, but it was another four weeks before I was able to drive and go back to work. I made it back for the start of school in September, though I wasn't clear of the symptoms from surgery. The lingering pain and side effects (more sweating) lasted the full year, but the operation worked. Cathy actually took over the draining procedure at school every day, so we found a routine that was not too disruptive. I questioned myself several times during that year whether or not this ordeal had been worthwhile, but it got slowly better until the sweating stopped and never came back. I would do it again if I had to.

August, 1998

I often used the term "vision" during the Fort years to describe the goals and type of climate I wanted to achieve. I was looking for some phrase or cause that would unite the members of our organization in an effort to inspire our performance. I had been challenged earlier in my career by a boss who asked me to define what it was about school in which I believed. I used that question to help define our vision and, therefore, direction. I'll never forget the fourth-grade girl who sat in the library one summer day and put into words the answer to my last question: What do I believe? I was talking to her mother, my great friend Brenda, who ran our library and was somewhat of an icon at the school, and asking her to help me define our school culture with something catchy that would get our student's attention. I asked the question, "What is it that we want?" Out of the mouths of babes came an answer . . .

"We want Fort Washington to be a place we want to come on Saturday!!" Young Miss Brittany Smith solved the riddle, and that quote appeared everywhere during my time there.

My life had come full circle and during this three-year period and with an assist from a nine-year-old girl, I answered the fourth and final question. I believed that my life's journey was worthy of living. Accomplishing things was important and I'd accomplished much of which I could be proud. If we don't have fun and fulfillment, though, what good is the reward that comes after you win or reach a goal? This young girl reminded me that the destination is not as important as the experience of getting there. In my life, Coach Bohan, my friends, and my family, made me believe in my existence and gave me hope for my personal journey. All the stuff about wins was a way to remind me that life was good and worth living. In that context, I learned that though my experience was different than I intended, my journey was worthy of completing. In fact, I knew I was enjoying life and that was what was important.

September, 1998

I knew at some point why I wanted to be a leader. As a teacher, I could impact my students in my classroom. From the principal's office, I had the opportunity to have an impact on a larger culture. If I wanted my kids, parents, and staff to have the type of educational opportunities that made us all want to come on Saturdays, the people had to matter. We had to care about each other to make our students' school experience memorable. All the adults had to be willing to create an environment where we enjoyed working if we wanted to be successful. The winners of such an environment were our kids because when our hearts are full and we believe what we are doing, we can really love our students. One day, near the end of my tenure at Fort Washington, Cathy and I were laughing at something and she started making fun of me. I laughingly told her that "I didn't feel her love," and she got a kick out of that. From then on, a running joke at our school always was "Hey Boss, do you feel the love, yet?" In a short time, I became the 'Feel The Love' guy, and I knew that I had accomplished what I wanted for that school. We put the fun back in school and solved a lot of other issues, including rebuilding trust.

I knew during my third year that I was ready for the next part of the journey. I started talking to my friend Steve and told him that I wanted to get back to the high school level and would love to be the principal at Clovis West when Gary was done. He wasn't going anytime soon, so I wasn't in a hurry. Earlier, my superintendent Walt had told me that a new high school was going to open, but I had worked at a new school once before and that was plenty, or so I thought. Steve and I would talk about my future regularly and I was prepared to wait until it was my turn and try to go back to CW. I honestly laughed about the prospect of becoming the first principal of what would become Clovis East High School until Steve said something interesting. He talked about the opportunity to really shape something as significant as a public high school that would be around for generations. We had large, successful high schools in our school district that were the focal points in our community. Each had cultures that were unique and provided great experiences for their students. As bad as I wanted to be a part of those cultures, he reminded me that the new school afforded me an incredible opportunity to create something from scratch that would be a reflection of me. The more I thought about it, the better it sounded and I applied when the interviews started in December.

There were eight of us who applied, and after a large panel interview made up of district and community members, I made the final four. The next day was an interview with the administrator in charge of the new area (the job equivalent to Steve) and she would narrow the field to two. When she called me to inform me that I was in the final pair, my gut told me it was my time. Sure enough, after another round of interviews the next day, I got the call and was named Clovis East's first principal.

There was much I didn't know. I knew it was going to be different but I didn't know what that meant. I knew I was drawing from a community that had a lot of ethnic diversity and large number of families impacted by poverty. I was immediately aware that students were not going to be happy about not attending the school they grew up cheering for. We were going to open with only freshman, but all of their school lives had been spent preparing to go to Clovis High, my alma mater. So, I had to convince them that our school would provide them the same experiences they were counting on, and I had no idea how I would do that. Finally, I had six months to convince enough teachers to leave their comfortable classrooms for an unknown. That, too, was something I had no idea how to accomplish.

188

I did know a couple of things, though. Clovis East would need to be built around its own culture that would be unique, focus on relationships, and make school an experience that our graduates would remember. High schools are important places in the lives of teenagers. Often, though, what is important to kids is not necessarily only the business of taking classes and graduating. They enjoy going to games, being with friends, and having pride in their school, and I wanted my kids to feel like they belonged to a place that they could cheer about. I started to wonder if perhaps my biggest contribution would be defining this thing called culture for my new school. So, I set about trying to find a catchy little slogan or phrase that would serve as an identifiable representation of Clovis East. Also, I wanted the culture to reflect what I thought was important. So, I wrote down some ideas until I flashed on one that I immediately knew was right: Clovis East High School . . . Feel The Love. The dream was on and I was in for a wild next few years. That much I knew for sure.

Of all the interviews I've been through, I'm pretty sure this was the first time my disability was never mentioned. I felt good about that because I really believed I'd answered any concern about my ability to produce at the necessary level. Certainly there was room for debate on who was the best qualified person to get the job, but my disability shouldn't have played into the argument. If nothing else, I think I'd put that to rest. I was pretty well known by this time in my career and thought everybody had made their peace with that part of my life . . . apparently not.

I immediately heard criticisms from all over. People complained I was too young and just got the job because I was a token. I didn't know until I got this job, but there had been whispering behind my back about my quick rise up the ladder. I heard from friends that a couple of people suggested that my career path was helped by the

189

attention I received for overcoming a disability. I heard complaints that I had nearly died during my recent bladder surgery and wasn't healthy enough. I also was immediately featured on television and in the paper as this unusual guy who beat the odds and, you know the rest. I was a little disappointed in all of that since I'd lived through those stories when I became a teacher. I was hoping that I had eliminated the notion that my career was a novelty and society should expect and encourage all of its citizens to find their place. I certainly had no complaints about where I was in life, but the attention being focused again on my chair didn't give me much reason to believe I had changed the stereotype of handicapped people in the workplace. For that I was bummed.

In the first couple of months, though, there was so much work to do it was insane. I got the job in December and had to finish the year at my elementary school. On one hand, I was glad because I wanted to complete the year for our sixth-grade kids to whom I'd grown pretty close. Also, my daughter was in second grade and could finish her year without too much disruption. At the same time, I had teachers to hire, uniforms to order, classes to schedule, and the minor dilemma of a huge high school that wasn't even built yet. There was a new intermediate school opening that would be part of our complex and that facility was completed first. Their principal and staff was hired at the same time I was, so the plan for me was to occupy a part of that campus for the first year and move into the beautiful new buildings in the fall of 2000, which would be our second year in existence. This idea was perfect since I would begin with about five hundred freshman who would become Clovis East's first graduates. The new intermediate school would send me their students each year and it would be four years before we had a full high school. So, I was in a four-year process of continual change that guaranteed a lot of sleepless nights.

By now, my secretary, Cathy, had become my most trusted colleague, and she and I got busy. We opened with nineteen teachers and four hundred seventy-three of the most culturally and economically diverse students ever brought together on one campus in our district. Clovis has always been a very conservative community with a population that is largely white and middle class. Our school was only fifty percent Caucasian with another twenty-five percent of our students being Hispanic. Since our town is in the heart of the San Joaquin Valley, we have a lot of farms and fields. As a result, our area has attracted many Southeast Asian families who come to work in farming. Our school would house the largest concentration of Hmong students ever in our district. Making up twenty percent of our school population, we knew the Hmong community would consider us their school, and they did.

August, 1999

On the day we opened, our students brought
with them varied experiences in school. When we looked
at test results on the academic records of our first group
of students, almost seventy percent couldn't read at grade
level. Many of them had never been on teams or been a
part of performing groups. School had not been a friendly
place for a large portion of our clientele and our community didn't come in with a great deal of trust in education,
so they certainly had little faith that a young school in its
first year could provide the best opportunities for kids.
We had no credibility, and it felt like we were actually
starting at whatever comes before square one.

As a group, our small staff fed off of the energy of being
pioneers and promised each other that we would close the
achievement gap and change the world for our students.
Our plan was to love them and create an experience that
allowed them to do things they didn't think were possible
for themselves. The work was going to be hard and frustrating for students and staff alike, so staying positive
was critically important. We were certain that we could
foster a belief in each student and teacher that success
was within their reach. I remembered Coach Bohan's
incessant "How many wins have you had today?" rheto-
ric and knew that would be a critical value that I could
utilize, and so our staff members promised each other we
would always take the time to celebrate all of the good
things that happen in our work. In fact, we began each
staff meeting with an opportunity for everybody to share
little victories that they experienced. That practice continues today and serves as a constant reminder that we
are fortunate to work with our students. All I asked of
our initial group of teachers was to build relationships

with their students that would be so strong that they would grieve at our graduation when we had to say good-bye. That seemed like a long time away, but it was the focal point of our work.

If we were going to have any academic success, we had to be able to teach our kids to read, a tough task with teen-agers. A struggling reader will have trouble in every dis-cipline, so we had to find instructional practices that were innovative and effective, and we aren't necessarily trained at the secondary level for that type of instruction. Moti-vation was critical, and I thought our students would try harder if they participated in activities outside of class. We wanted to create opportunities for our young people to participate in sports, the arts, agriculture, and any other programs that would make their school experience more fun. Many of our students had not been in situations where they were able to be a part of high profile groups, but they would be here. We even adopted a schedule with eight class periods as opposed to the typical six to force students to take elective classes. Finally, I wanted kids to feel safe and was concerned about how well our different cultures would interact with each other. It seemed natu-ral to use our diversity as an on-going tool to teach inclu-sion, social tolerance and justice, and caring. So, we took our Feel The Love motto and defined it with three words: Competence, Connectedness, and Compassion. These words combined our goals of helping students achieve academically, provide them a sense of belonging, and cre-ate an environment where we care about each other. We put those words on a poster and hung them in every room and office in the school. It became who we were and caught on quickly. Two of my colleagues even gave us the nickname of "The Love Shack" and our marching band still plays the song as a way of celebrating our identity.

The first year was humbling and much harder than we had dreamed. The academic work was very different and we all had to begin a training regimen to learn new instructional strategies. I had to scramble to try and finance the opportunities that we wanted to provide. The biggest challenge, however, was to try and make our small, freshman only group feel as though they were as good as anyone else. More to the point, we had to sell them on the idea that their high school experience was as valid as their friends at other schools. This proved amazingly difficult and was compounded by the fact that our school had to grow up in the shadows of three of the finest high school institutions in the state. We plodded along, though, and tried to make a huge deal out of every success, no matter how small.

One moment stands out in the first year. I was concerned about our Southeast Asian students. I met with a group of them and they shared with me that they felt very isolated. They told me of incidents where kids called them "Gooks" and "cat-eaters." I could easily see that they were feeling the sting of prejudice and discrimination. One day, a group of Hmong dancers were performing on our amphitheater stage and I noticed some movement in the crowd. A few boys started walking around the area picking up friends and creating a stir. As this pack of young men grew, they started in my direction. As they approached, you could see they were agitated and wanted to talk.

They looked at me and one of them asked, "When do we get to have White Pride Day?" I knew at that moment that Feel The Love was going to be an on-going learning process. Racism exists everywhere, and apparently our school was no exception. It became more important than ever to talk about social tolerance.

In spite of all the work we did with "wins," the hardest part of the first couple of years was staying positive. It was way too easy to get consumed in the trials and tribulations of the daily grind and we found ourselves often complaining about anything possible. Our core group of staff did a great job of maintaining that spirit, but it got tougher to maintain as time went on. Every year we added a new grade level of students and another group of staff members. Some of our staff came to our school because they wanted to; others were transferred against their will. They didn't want to even try to embrace the new things we were trying, and they certainly didn't share in the enthusiasm of being at a new school. It was like starting over each fall and having to constantly defend your belief system. I was way out there anyway with the whole love thing so I was a pretty easy target. Even though we had moved into our new facility, there wasn't total harmony. I learned quickly that debating naysayers was pointless. Nothing I said convinced the unhappy folks that we had a good school and a good climate. Some of the teachers who came to us by force actually said that they were going to try to do everything in their power to mess us up. They badmouthed our school to the kids, which still amazes me. The only way I knew to endure this type negativity was to scream your beliefs at the top of your lungs from every rooftop available and not allow yourself to be compromised on the core values of your organization. The more I talked about how good we were, the more people believed it. I'm not sure if that worked, but I felt better. In my lifetime, I had faced bigger challenges, and I was willing to deal with another. The good news was our school continued to grow and prosper and I think that our belief system was the reason we made it through the tough times.

September, 2001

I will forever remember the beginning of this
school year as the time we arrived. To be sure, we were
still struggling to find our wins, but on one Friday afternoon, shortly after the start of our third year in existence,
our students became a community. A few days earlier,
we watched in horror with the rest of the world as terror
struck the World Trade Center on September 11th. Our
staff, like everyone else in the world, struggled to make
sense of this to our kids. Our students wanted to talk
about it and we spent a week together trying to come to
terms with our fears and insecurities. We weren't unique
in the need to do something, and student groups were
trying to be busy and participate in projects that could
offer some help to the victims. The President had called
for a national moment of silence for Friday and our school
would certainly participate. I heard of elaborate plans to
commemorate the moment, but that didn't seem real, so I
opted to pass on a fancy ceremony.

I didn't plan the moment, but that is probably why it
happened. I got on the school public address system on
Friday morning and said that we'd join President Bush
at noon for the moment of silence. I added as an aside
that I was going to observe the time in the amphitheater
on the lawn and invited anyone who wanted to join me.
If you have been responsible for supervising a group of
fifteen hundred teenagers, you realize how stupid that
was. At noon, however, I rolled out into the middle of the
large, open space and sat in silence in a daze over the
magnitude of this event. I was unprepared for what happened next. I looked up and students and teachers were
pouring out of their classrooms by the hundreds. Nobody said a word, but in a matter of a couple of minutes,

I was surrounded by our entire student and adult population. We sat together for over twenty minutes in total silence. The power of that gathering was the single most overwhelming experience of unity of which I'd ever been a part. I had goose bumps, to say the least. Near the end, a young girl stood up and walked to the front of the crowd. She dropped to her knees in prayer and I remember being struck by her courage. Soon, students began following her lead until we had the entire crowd together, arms around one another, in total silence. It was incredible and the proudest I'd ever been of a group of young people in my life. I told them that and went to lunch, but we grew up as an institution that day. I also found out that our students knew about the word 'love.'

We had enjoyed some successes in places like the performing arts and agriculture, but we had two big athletic successes that brought some pride to our student body in that third year. Without a senior class and playing with juniors as our older group, we were constantly at a competitive disadvantage and finding wins was really difficult. Two groups broke through and really provided some hope. Our girls cross country won the Valley championship, a remarkable accomplishment for such a young program. As amazing or more, we fielded our first varsity football team and they managed to make the section playoffs. The significance for us was that our games brought together parents and community, our cheerleaders, marching band and student rooters, for the first time, to cheer for Clovis East High School. To the surprise of everyone, we won our first two playoff games and found ourselves playing for the section championship. To the best of anyone's recollection, we were the first team ever in California to play for a section title without a senior class. We lost the final game, but we had fun and our school was enjoying its first momentum, and we rode it as long as we could. Still, we were ready for the building process to end and we desperately needed to feel as though we were equal to the other schools.

August, 2002

You could feel the breath of fresh air on our campus as we opened our fourth year. We had seniors, and these young men and women had been through so much growth, they deserved a great senior year. Our culture was thriving and I still was spreading my message ad nauseum. We had built so much of our hopes over the years on the first graduation, and it was now very close and we could taste it. This was to be our validation, and we needed to know that we had accomplished this milestone. The painful building process would become totally worthwhile when our students started receiving acceptance letters to major colleges and universities. I had this reoccurring nightmare that we would get close to the climactic moment of this huge professional undertaking and the governor would show up and declare that we forgot something and everyone had to start over. Mercifully, UC Davis, Cal, and Fresno State, just to name a few came to the rescue and convinced our students that we had been telling the truth. As a staff, we never felt like we came up with any magical solutions, but we had certainly seen a lot of growth in our students' skills. The whole year was a celebration of the victory of feeling like we were finally worthy. Though our football team was ranked number one most of the year, we had our hearts broken in the playoffs and didn't get that huge win on a public stage. Still, we were a proud bunch as we prepared for the graduation ceremony that was so important to a lot of folks. I was particularly pleased when the local newspaper ran a story and interviewed many of our kids about the feelings associated with being the first graduating class. The things that were important to them were learning how to be good to each other. It was funny because the one thing everybody knew was the phrase "Feel The Love." I think they even knew what it meant because the person they elected to speak on their behalf at the ceremony was a young Hmong woman; White Pride Day was a long forgotten thought.

We did have two major marquee moments that occurred within days of each other. One week, we took a group of choir students to perform at the Lincoln Center in New York, where they won a gold medal. Many had never flown, and some had never seen snow. All of them got to experience something they'd never forget and helped them see the potential that exists outside what they already knew. Later that week, a group of our percussionists competed in the World Championships in Dayton, Ohio. They had qualified by winning regional competitions throughout the spring and were just proud to be able to participate in this event. I was doubly proud because I got to enjoy this event as a principal and a father. When I made the move to open the new school, I brought Jared with me. I was concerned about him and wanted him close and it had paid off. He had always been a great student, but had trouble fitting in. His social skills were not great, but I figured that he just hadn't found a group of students with which he shared a common interest. His life changed quickly for the better when he joined the band. Jared was a piano player and quickly became known as a fine musician. Besides the keyboard, he was pretty skilled on the percussion instruments, and he was a critical part of the group. We never imagined winning, but we did. To hear Clovis East and World Champions in the same breath was probably more than I had a right to expect, but it sounded good.

As graduation day arrived, I was overcome with professional pride mixed with a hint of sadness over saying goodbye to a group of young people I loved and owed so much. I couldn't help being struck by the similarities of this moment to my own high school experience. My graduation was filled with the sense that I had overcome a lot to be on that stage. There were days of fear and doubt, but I had arrived on that platform with great hope for the future in spite of what had happened to me. I had been given a gift of love and I wasn't going to waste it. Now, twenty-five years later, I sat in the same stadium on the same stage. Our school shared Clovis High School's facility, so everything was strangely familiar. I was joined this time by four hundred people that had lived for four years as the underdog and faced their share of doubt. They, too, were filled with hope and had received the gift of love. The difference for me was that I was the giver this time, and I was damned proud. I faced the crowd of some ten thousand happy family members and conferred upon this group their diplomas. And I left the stage and unleashed a lifetime of tears. We had done it, and it felt really good.

We hadn't had that big moment in front of everyone else, but we were winners in our own eyes, and that was the most important thing. Still, it would have been nice to have a little time to bask in the public light. Hopefully, it would happen for us someday soon. Sure enough, the next fall, it was only one play away.

November, 2003

*I*t was *third and five.* As the ball was snapped, the silence on our side of the field was deafening. Our junior quarterback spun around, faked a handoff, tucked the ball and headed up field. We had run this play a lot over the season, but not with this much on the line. My heart sank when he was hit hard after about a three-yard gain leaving him short of the magical first down. The eruption on our sideline startled me and I realized that Westy had stayed on his feet and staggered forward. He finally fell and the ball was spotted by the referee. His second effort was good enough for a seven-yard gain and a Clovis East first down. We knew this game was over. We snapped the ball twice more and Zach, a senior who came in to replace Westy for the final plays, knelt down as the clock ticked to zero. As Diana Ross' voice hit the speakers, she was joined by a chorus of thousands who deliriously sang "Ain't No Mountain High Enough" in full voice. Our team doused our coach with the obligatory water bucket and I broke out in an goofy jig on the track by our sideline. The bedlam would last and reached a fever pitch when the coach and I were called to the middle of the field and presented with a plaque with the words CIF CENTRAL SECTION CHAMPIONS across the front. WE WERE WINNERS!

Our crowd poured onto the middle of the field. There were non-stop hugs, high fives, and pats on the back. There were tears from kids and adults alike that suggested this moment was bigger than just a football game. I'm not sure I can explain why or even justify the fact that it was that big of a deal, but I felt it too. On the surface, we were all happy that we won and incredibly proud of our coaches and players. On the inside was something greater than that; there was a pride in this win that comes only when you have been at the bottom and accomplished something that didn't seem possible. So many of us savored this victory because it was a symbol of what we wanted our lives to represent. Our school community matched an unlikely group of people. We were a group from all walks of life and at varying stages of our own struggles. At that moment, though, in the middle of that field in the chill of November, we were a family; and we were all CHAMPIONS. This time, everybody knew it.

I happened to live near the stadium and wheeled myself the short distance down the road to my house. My colleague, Barry, and I hardly spoke as we moved through the darkness toward the victory party that waited inside my front door. I took these few minutes and tried to soak it all in. It had been a life-changing ride and it was pretty poignant. My father would lose his battle with cancer in the months ahead and the Eben family would gather in sadness. I'm sure our students and their families would all face more battles and challenges as their individual and collective journeys would continue. We all had something in common, though. We finally knew what it was like to be a champion, and we all got to dance the elusive victory dance. Coach Bohan wasn't there that night, but if he was, I know I would have grabbed that plaque and rolled up to him and shouted, "Hey Coach, how many wins did YOU have today?"

EPILOGUE

• In 2007, I lost my beloved Coach. After making such an amazing difference in the lives of thousands of young people, his heart gave out on a family vacation at the far too young age of 69. In an incredible irony to me, he was water- skiing at the time of his death. I gave the eulogy at his packed funeral service and promised his family that I would continue telling his story of hope, love, and counting your blessings every day. His influence on my life can never be measured and I am so grateful that I was able to tell him that I loved him.

• About the same time, I left education and spent four years in municipal government. I was named Deputy Mayor of Fresno and, though completely out of my element, had a blast working on city-wide issues. I even ran for Mayor in 2008; I didn't win but had an awesome time and finished 4th in a field of eleven. It was the best of times and the worst of times as I learned a lot and felt really alive during the campaign. I took a beating, though, in the media and couldn't mount a serious threat. They saw me as an outsider and not worthy of consideration. I met some great people, though, along the way including Governor Arnold Schwarzenegger and a bombastic New York developer and his daughter who were interested in buying a golf course in the area. It was fun talking with them, but it didn't seem too important . . . Until later when the pair hit the news fairly regularly after changing jobs. We should have worked harder to close a deal with Donald and Ivanka Trump. I closed my time in government working as the CEO of the Fresno Convention and Visitors Bureau. Destination Marketing and the small team we had assembled turned out to be the most enjoyable work experience I'd ever known, and you haven't lived until your livelihood depends on selling Fresno as a tourist destination.

• I'm sad to say that Michelle and I divorced after 27 years of marriage in 2009. We had become distant and I felt like I needed to leave the relationship. It was awful and we didn't do well for a long time. I'm happy to say that we get along pretty well now and continue to co-parent our kids, even as they are adults. Michelle continues to work as an accountant in Fresno and enjoys a great relationship with our kids and the new man in her life.

• Jared and Noelle have become wildly successful scholars and are settling into adult life. Jared's ability to play the piano created opportunities to earn his Bachelor's and Master's Degree in Piano Performance. He is in his early stages of Doctoral studies and has become a marvelous musician, composer, and first class dude. Noelle literally traveled the world to earn her Bachelor's and Master's Degrees. In the field of global studies, she has become a human rights advocate and a passionate protector of citizenship and culture around the globe. She has been a constant source of protection for me, even though she isn't crazy about the time she has spent being my caretaker and rock. Without question, these 2 are my greatest joys, my best friends, and my biggest wins in a life that has been full of wins.

• As for me, my journey continues to be exciting, unpredictable, and full of great and not-so-great moments. I've had opportunities to do some really cool things and have been humbled by the realities of life. After my divorce, I followed a former high school sweetheart to the beautiful state of Wisconsin. I spent a year as principal of a high performing elementary school and met some of the best teachers with whom I've ever worked. I yearned for a different challenged, though, and asked to be moved to a large urban high school name JI Case. The school was failing by every measure and the staff and students had given up.

I spent the most significant three years of my professional life working to rebuild that culture. Our students came alive and our staff followed suit. In fact, I discovered that the educators were really superstars waiting to be supported and given the opportunity to shine. We became a team, and I could literally see the improvement in every area. Academics, the Arts, and Athletics got better. We saw big attendance improvements and the discipline environment became much more pleasant. I left there incredibly proud of the work.

• The relationship was less successful. The former girlfriend and I spent a great first year together and discovered the unbelievable cool of Milwaukee, Wisconsin. I loved the city, the architecture, the nightlife, and even the snow. I thought, at least for a while, I was in heaven. As fate would have it, time spoiled the relationship and it became unbearable. I split from her after 3 tumultuous years and started to realize that I am not winning in the relationship arena. I've had a couple since then, nut nothing that has lasted, unfortunately for me.

• I'd probably still be in Wisconsin if not for a medical procedure gone wrong that almost killed me. I went in to have a small hemorrhoid removed, an outpatient surgery that lasted a couple of hours. I was home by dinner and back to work in a day. During the weekend, I went to a drama festival with students and felt strange all day. By Sunday I was sweating profusely and chilled to the bone. Over the next year, I was in and out of the hospital, tested for everything, and placed on every medication known to man. Nothing stopped the sweating. In addition, I was having massive bowel movements in my pants every day. I was in and out of work and mostly housebound for a year. The doctor threw up his hands in June and had me take a disability retirement. So, that was it...I left my job and Wisconsin and returned to California to be near family.

207

• I decided to seek a second opinion in California. The surgeon in Los Angeles performed a Colostomy, and that worked wonders. As surgeries go, it went well and I had very little pain. I wear a pouch now to go to the bathroom which is pretty unpleasant. It stopped the problem of random accidents, though, so life was able to continue. I recovered at my brother's house for several months, but am healthy again and ready to go.

• Being out of work for the better part of a year convinced me of one simple truth; I have no desire to retire. I wanted to return to the workplace and, after an unsuccessful attempt to work at a Charter school, I bet on myself. I thought it was time to fulfill a promise I made and have devoted my life to sharing my story and Coach Bohan's message. After 30 years in education, speaking gives me joy and meaning. I am right where I need to be. I never wanted to be alone, but it has worked out that way, and I'm ok. So, it's me, my kids, and my story . . . pretty good WINS today.